ONCE UPON A TIME

LIFE HAPPENED

Joan Gasperson

Dedication

I dedicate this book to Ms. Abbie Dunn, our church librarian and retired school teacher. She spent countless hours editing my book for me. Thank you, Abbie. May God richly bless and keep you.

CONTENTS

Foreword	7
Only One Way	9
Whatever It Takes	29
Rich Though Poor	47
Jailed But Free	78
The Consequences of Choices	99
Until Death We Do Part	127
Never Too Old	168
Mansion On A Hill	174
Note from Author	179

FOREWORD

"Once upon a time", these are words that we often heard our parents read to us when we were children. Once upon a time there was a young girl named Cinderella or something like that. These stories always had happy endings. The good guys always won out in the end. We all know that they were not true to life but they made us feel good.

We girls all wanted to be the beautiful princess who gets swept away by the handsome prince.

When we became adults, we left the fairy tales behind us. We all know that there are no fairy godmothers, no handsome princes or beautiful princesses, and no pumpkins that turn into carriages. We aren't looking for fables and fairy tales; we are looking for answers to help us in the real life.

That is the purpose of this book of short stories. In it you will read about families with some of the same problems that we are going through or have gone through.

They aren't true stories, they are fictional, but they are true to life. They have a message. All of my stories are based on Christian principles.

Remember in the Bible when Jesus spoke in parables. They were earthly stories with heavenly meanings.

That could well describe this book. I take life situations that very likely could have happened and show how God's grace and mercy can change things.

Some of the stories have happy endings, some may not, but all will direct you to the one who can make a difference in your life.

They may make you cry at times. My greatest desire is that you be encouraged, challenged, and yes, even convicted if need be. They are earthly stories with a heavenly purpose. I hope you enjoy reading them

Joan Gasperson.

ONLY ONE WAY

There is a way that seems right unto a man, but its end is the way to death. Proverbs 16:25

Jesus said unto him, I am the way, the truth, and the life, no man comes unto the Father except through me. John 14:6

Barry Norman walked down the hall of the Political Science building at the University of South Florida. He could not believe that he was finally here. It was a dream come true.

He had been home schooled by his mother.

The home schooling program in which they had been involved had a scholarship program. This program had been set up by an anonymous donor so bright students, such as himself, would be able to go to the best schools.

Barry had scored higher than anyone on all his test scores.

It was his desire to go into politics. He felt that there just were not enough good moral politicians in government anymore. He hoped that he would be able to bring Christian ideals back into government. He knew it would not be easy but he felt he had to try.

His last class of the morning was with Professor Brown. He had heard a lot about this professor. He was an atheist and he liked to antagonize those students who claim to believe in God, especially Christians. He would always manage to weave an assignment into the curriculum that would offer him an opportunity to refute any of their beliefs.

Barry was not looking forward to this class but he had to have it to get his degree.

Barry and his family were Christians. The Norman kids were well grounded in their faith and knew what they believed, but would they be able to stand against the ridicule and pressure of a staunch atheistic professor.

He and his parents had prayed fervently over just this issue. They wanted him to be able to give a clear descriptive answer as to why he believed what he believed.

Barry meditated on such scriptures as; **I Pet 3:15; But sanctify the Lord God in your hearts, and always be ready to give a defense to everyone who asks you a reason for the hope that is in you, with meekness and fear; and Luke 12:11-12 "Now when they bring you to the synagogues and magistrates and authorities, do not worry about how or what you should answer, or what you should say. For the Holy Spirit will teach you in that very hour what you ought to say."** These scriptures gave him courage to face the world and lean on his faith that God would keep His word.

He still was not looking forward to the classes with Prof. Brown. Today's class would be the third class that he had had with Prof. Brown. So far he had not said or done anything that caused any of the students a problem, but he knew that would soon change.

Prof. Brown stood up before the class. "Ladies and gentlemen, you very well know if you go into politics you need to be able to argue your case and convince others to follow your point of view."

"The rule of thumb in today's politics is the separation of church and state. I know that many of you believe in some kind of God. Your assignment tomorrow is to write an argument as to what your stand on this particular issue is. Then present your argument before the class, me in particular, convincing us why your view is true."

Since we have people of different faiths in this class, include in your argument why you think your way is the best way."

The professor looked over the class with a smirk on his face. He then dismissed the students.

They were all whispering regarding the assignment that he had just given. They knew that Prof. Brown prided himself in breaking the spirit of many of his students.

Since it was his last class for the day, Barry went to his dorm room to begin his paper.

First he called his parents.

He explained to his parents about the assignment his professor had given them. He asked them to request prayer for him when they went to Bible study that night.

His parents prayed for him over the phone and assured him that others would be praying also.

He knelt down by his bed and prayed for guidance.

He got up off of his knees and went over to his desk, got out his laptop and pulled up the word program.

He began typing. At the top of the page he wrote; **One Nation Under God.**

Although he was well versed in the history of the United States, he spent time researching his information. He wanted to be accurate in his argument, leaving no room for rebuttal

When he finished that section he began the next section, **Only One Way**.

It was late when he finished His paper.

He knelt down and said another prayer and went to bed.

His first classes the next day went smoothly. Then it came time for his last class with Prof. Brown.

He sat and listened intently as each student presented their case before the class. Then it was his turn.

He began, "I believe according to recorded history that the United States of America was founded on Christian principles.

It was the intention of our forefathers to establish a nation where people would have the freedom to worship their God in whatever way they saw fit.

I would like to site some passages from our most sacred documents to back up my argument.

One such passage can be found in the Declaration of Independence. **" We hold these truths to be self-evident, that all men are created equal, that they are endowed by <u>their Creator with certain unalienable Rights;</u> that among these are Life, Liberty and the pursuit of Happiness."**

Our forefathers believed in one God who created heaven and earth. They believed in the right of man to call upon that God without fear of a tyrant king forcing his beliefs on them.

They concluded the declaration with, **"And for the support of this Declaration, with a firm reliance on <u>the protection of Divine Providence, we mutually pledge to each other our Lives, our Fortunes, and our sacred Honor.</u>"**

There were 56 men who signed this declaration. Some lost their lives, some came to adverse poverty. They were willing to give their lives because of their belief in God.

They desired that this country be founded on Christian principles and did not want a government that would hinder anyone in any way from practicing their beliefs. So when they wrote the Constitution they included in the Bill of Rights the following amendment; **"Congress shall make no law respecting an establishment of religion, or prohibiting the free exercise thereof; or abridging the freedom of speech, or of the press; or the right of the people peaceably to assemble, and to petition the Government for a redress of grievances."**

They never intended that our government be devoid of belief in God but that man would have the right to choose whether or not he wanted to believe.

The laws of this land were based on Biblical teachings, the Ten Commandments in particular.

The curriculum used in the schools was based on Biblical principles. The Bible was often used as a textbook.

The direction of our nation changed in the early 1960's, beginning with the time when an atheistic woman convinced the Supreme Court that prayer didn't belong in the schools.

Since that time things have gone downhill. Crime and violence have increased.

A nation that was once rich in its own resources has become dependent on foreign resources.

A nation that once was a leader in the world is increasingly sliding down hill to certain destruction.

We elected a president who does not even honor the American flag, or the men who fought and died for our freedom. He refused to take part in the National Day of Prayer because he was afraid that he might offend someone. Yet he knelt with the Muslims at the capitol building. Was he not afraid of offending Christians?

We now have a nation that is on the brink of destruction.

I must summarize my stand with a verse from the Bible. **Ps 9:17; The wicked shall be turned into hell, And all the nations that forget God.**

May God help our nation to turn back to Him."

Barry continued, "I believe we can learn from history, if we do not try to change what is written, as our modern day historians have attempted to do."

There are many views about who God is and how we get to Him.

We are told in today's world that there are many ways to God. We just have to be tolerant. I beg to differ, but in order to clarify my stand let's take a look at the three major religions of the world, Christianity, Muslim, and Hinduism.

First we have the Muslim faith. This religion was founded by the prophet Mohammed, who died around 632 and is buried in a tomb that can be visited today.

In the Koran, which is their holy scriptures, they are told to kill the infidels, meaning Jews and

Christians. They are not told to love them and convert them.

They believe that if they martyr themselves by killing Jews and Christians they will have a special place in heaven.

They believe that you get to heaven by doing good deeds and obeying the Holy Koran.

The Hindu faith has many different belief systems. Some believe in only one God while others have over 300,000. They believe that the mind is the essence of all things and that when one dies their spirit goes out of the top of their head and rests for a while in the nothingness of space until it is allowed to come back through reincarnation. They also believe that since the mind is the essence of all things whatever you were thinking at the point of death has a lot to do with the state of life you find yourself in when you come back.

Some believe that you come back as another person, while others believe you can come back as plants and animals. Some refrain from eating meat because of this, especially the sacred cow.

They believe that all low life comes back as low life and remain low life. The higher realm of people keep coming back until they get it right, then they can go to where the ultimate god is.

Orthodox Hindus believe you are born a Hindu and do not try to convert others to their religion.

They are very harsh on those of their faith that convert to Christianity.

There have been more Christians martyred for their faith in the past 30 years than all the years prior throughout history.

If you compare these religions with other religions of the world, they are all work based. They try to outweigh the bad with the good.

In the final analysis how they live their lives has a lot to do with what kind of afterlife they have.

All religions are trying to find God or a higher being by their own efforts."

Barry took a long deep breath and continued, "I believe in a loving, gracious, merciful God. I believe that He is the only God and that there is only one way that we can even kneel before His Holy presence

Christianity is far different from any other religions.

God in His infinite mercy and grace seeks out man.

The Christian believes in one God, who manifests Himself as the Father, the Son, and the Holy Spirit.

We believe that He is the creator of all things. He created the heavens and the earth and all things in it. He created man in His own image. Man did not just evolve from some lower animal form.

We hold to the truth of God's word that man is a sinner and that because of his sin he is separated from God.

God from the very beginning knew what man would do and planned to send His Son to atone for the sins of mankind.

God loved His creation and wanted us to love Him back. The Bible says, **"He who knew no sin, became sin so we could be brought back to the Father."**

He suffered on a cruel cross at the hands of angry sinners so that the world could be saved.

The only condition for salvation is that they believe and trust in the wonderful mercy and grace of God through His Son.

Works cannot earn anyone acceptance with a Holy God. So Jesus died, was buried and rose again so that man could be saved. Jesus is not dead. History records eye witnesses to His resurrection. Over 500 persons saw Him after His resurrection.

I hold these things to be true for the following reasons:

The first evidence is the Holy Scriptures.. Jesus said in **John 14:6; "I am the way, the truth, and the life; no man comes to the Father except through Me."** Jesus is who He said He is or He is the biggest liar to ever walk earth's surface. He is either the only way or there is no way at all.

The second piece of evidence is my own testimony and the countless testimonies of millions of others as to what faith and trust in Him has done in our lives.

My evidence may not be conclusive to you but if I am wrong I have nothing to lose. If you are wrong you have everything to lose.

I hope you will give much thought to what I have said today. It is a matter of life or death.

Barry handed his paper to professor and went to his seat.

He picked up Barry's paper. There was something different about this work. True it lacked the style and form that a seasoned debater would have, but something was different about it.

He knew that this paper deserved an A+ but he could not lose face in front of his whole class, plus he was unwilling to concur that there was a God.

Yet deep inside he knew he had just lied, something about this paper touched a raw nerve. He placed a big D right in the middle of the paper. Everyone else received an F.

The next day he handed out the papers.

There were gasps from those he had given F's, but they had nothing to say.

He handed Barry his paper. Barry shook his head in amazement.

He did not remain quiet as the others had. "I don't understand," he said. "I did as you requested. Why did I only get a D?"

Prof. Brown retorted, "Young man your assignment was to convince me that there was a

God. You have failed to do this. I should have given you an F. The only way I will believe in God is if He strikes me down when I leave this hall this afternoon and I am sure that is not going to happen."

Barry was standing outside the hall when the professor came out. He was on the phone with his parents and had told them what the professor had said to him. "I have such a burden for this man. I would be willing to do anything if he would come to know our Lord."

He and his parents prayed over the phone that God would convict the heart of the professor no matter what it took.

He walked over to curb where the professor was about to cross the road. The professor turned as he walked over to him. He turned and said to Barry, "You see young man God has not struck me down. I guess you were wrong. There is no God."

He then, without looking, stepped down off the curb into the path of a speeding sports car, which was coming around the corner.

Barry ran into the road and pushed the professor out of the way just in time.

The car hit Barry knocking him several feet down the road.

The professor ran over to where Barry lay mangled and bleeding.

"Why did you do that?" he asked. "You could have proven your point."

Barry, in barely audible, tones said, "Then it would have been too late. Jesus loves you, Professor Brown. He doesn't just want you to believe he exists. He wants you to allow him to save you."

Barry died in the professor's arms.

Barry's funeral was set for the next week.

Professor Brown could not get Barry's essay or what he had said before he died out of his mind. He knew he had to go to the funeral.

The funeral was held in Barry's home church. There was standing room only. Student after student got up and told how Barry had influenced them to accept Christ.

His uncle, who was pastor of the church, got up to speak. "This is a sad time for all of us. Barry will be missed, but he would not want us to be sad. He is in heaven with our Lord. He would want me to tell those of you who are present about the love of Jesus and how you too can receive eternal life. That was the most important thing in his young life."

He went on to tell of the love and sacrifice of Jesus.

All the professor could think of was that Barry had also sacrificed his life for him. He had never seen such love and commitment in any of his students before.

Barry's uncle ended the service with an invitation for those who did not know Christ but would like to, to come forward. Professor Brown rose from his seat with tears streaming down his face and went forward and took the preacher's hand.

WHATEVER IT TAKES

Romans 12:12 Rejoice in hope; be patient in affliction; be persistent in prayer.
James 5:16 Confess your trespasses to one another, and pray for one another, that you may be healed. The effective, fervent prayer of a righteous man avails much.

"Daddy's home, daddy's home," shouted the little girl as she jumped from her usual perch in the living room window.

She ran to the door that led out to the garage. The garage door began to rise as her dad pulled up into the driveway.

Every day it was the same scene. Katie. an energetic child of five, waited for her Dad to come home.

She loved her Dad very much. He had always played with her when he first came home and she looked forward to it every day.

Something seemed different today. Her Dad wasn't smiling as he usually was. When he got out of the car, he hardly even gave her a notice.

The little girl's joyful face became sad. She pulled on his coat sleeve. Her dad looked down at her with a look that she had never seen before and said in a hateful tone, "Not now Katie, I have got a lot on my mind. Go to your room and play with your dolls."

Katie was heartbroken. She ran to her mother in the kitchen." Mommy something is wrong with daddy, he doesn't want to play with me."

Ellen bent down and hugged the little girl with the long blond curls and big blue eyes. "It will be okay, honey. Dad is just tired. Go to your room and get ready for supper."

Katie turned and went to her room with tears running down her little face.

Ellen and Rick had lived in this neighborhood for 10 years. They had married just out of high school and had been married for 15 years. They had waited a long time for Katie to come along. She was their pride and joy, especially to Rick. She was truly daddy's little girl. He dotted on her every whim.

Rick was a successful engineer, in a reputable engineering company. He made real good money, which made it possible for Ellen to stay at home with Katie. They truly lived the American ideal. They had everything they could ever want.

Rick at one time had felt called into the ministry. He and Ellen had been very active in youth group when they were teenagers. When they got married, the struggles of college life and everyday living just seemed to get in the way.

Ellen and Katie still attended a small church in town, but Rick just never seemed to have time. He had quit going a long time ago. He always used the excuse that you didn't have to go to church to worship God. It bothered Ellen, but she tried not to nag him. She just continued to go alone, because she felt it important that Katie learn about Jesus. Although she read Bible stories and prayed with her every day, she knew that the influence of other Christians was very important. Besides she also needed the encouragement of older more mature brothers and sisters in Christ.

She continued to pray for Rick and hoped that one day he would come back to the Lord. Besides everything seemed to be okay and all was well, or so she thought.

Ellen wiped her hands on the hand towel and laid it down. She went into the family room where Rick was slumped in the recliner. She could tell by the look on his face that something was wrong.

She sat down on the couch. She sat there for a moment expecting him to say something, but he didn't.

Finally she spoke up. "What is wrong? You broke Katie's heart."

Rick just stared at the floor. He didn't respond for a long time. Then he spoke up. "I was laid off today. The company is in financial trouble and they are closing their doors. "

Ellen let out a deep sigh. "Oh honey, I am so sorry. It will be okay. You are a good engineer. You will find a job. Even if we have to move, it will be okay. I can go back to work at the hospital."

With that Rick got up, and without saying a word, he went out the door.

Things began to change after that. Bills began to pile up. Creditors were calling on the phone all hours of the day. Ellen just stopped answering it and would let the answering machine pick up.

Although Rick was not happy about it, Ellen went back to work. She was a registered nurse and had stopped working to raise Katie. Of course, she couldn't match the salary that Rick had previously but at least she was able to catch up with most of the bills.

This didn't help matters with Rick. He didn't like the fact that she was working again and he wasn't.

He began to change. He was bitter and angry. All they did was fight and argue.

Rick began to blame God for all of their troubles.

Ellen could not understand this since Rick had not even acknowledged God for over 15 years. How could he blame God?

Ellen talked with her pastor and tried to get Rick to talk also, but he was a private man with a lot of pride.

He hated that Ellen was working and could not accept the fact that Ellen was now supporting them. That was the man's responsibility.

He could not admit to someone else that he needed help. He felt he could take care of it himself. But he wasn't taking care of it. He had put his resume in at every opportunity with no results. The economy was bad everywhere and the job market was way down. They were not the only ones in this situation.

Ellen did not know how much more she could take. She still loved Rick with all of her heart but he just wasn't the same man she had married. She did not know what she was going to do.

She didn't get much support from him. He resented the fact she was paying the bills. Their relationship had deteriorated. It had been a very long time since they had been intimate.

Divorce was out of the question. She had not only made a commitment to Rick, she had made a commitment to God. Besides she still loved Rick.

Ellen had always been a woman of prayer. So she prayed. Right now that was the only constant in her life.

She did not know what she would do if she did not have the Lord to lean on. She knew that he would hear her prayers in His time. It wasn't easy, this waiting game.

The greatest casualty to this tragedy was Katie. She couldn't understand why her mommy and daddy were always fighting. Her daddy never played with her anymore, no matter how much she pleaded.

Ellen and Katie continued to go to church.

Katie would always request prayer for her daddy. Although Katie was only 6, she had already accepted Jesus as her Savior. Ellen marveled at the faith in her little girl, she loved Jesus with all of her heart.

One evening during their bedtime prayers Katie ask if she could pray first. She began, "Jesus please help my daddy. Help him to go with us to church and help him find a job. I love my daddy so much and it makes me so sad to see him being so sad. I don't care what it takes; I just want my daddy to love me again and to love you also. Amen."

Ellen continued, "Yes Lord whatever it takes please bring Rick back to you and help us in our distress."

They did not realize what the outcome of what they had just prayed would be.

Ellen bent over and kissed Katie on her forehead. "I love you baby," she said.

She turned out the light and went into the family room where Rick sat in his lounge chair.

"Rick we need to talk," she said.

He didn't answer, so she began. "Rick, it has been a year since you lost your job. I know that you have done everything you possibly can to find a job. I know you resent me for working, but this is how it has to be right now. You should be thankful that I am able to do it. I am very concerned about how this is affecting our relationship and your care for Katie."

"You know I love you with all my heart and so does Katie. She prays for you all the time and her little heart is breaking. You have pushed us out of your life like it was our fault. You blame God for our troubles but you don't do anything to try and restore your relationship with Him. I don't know how much more we can take."

Ellen became silent waiting for a response from Rick.

Rick began, "Why should I trust a God who would allow all this to happen to us?"

Ellen could tell that there was no getting through to him. She got up and went to their bedroom.

Once again she knelt by her bed and prayed, "Lord, please whatever it takes cause Rick to come back to you. I trust in you to take care of us, and I know you will. Please Lord answer my prayer. Amen."

She got up, got in the bed and cried herself to sleep.

Rick continued to search for a job. Finally after being out of work for over a year and a half he received a call from an engineering company not far from where they lived.

The compensation was not the same as his previous job but there was room for growth and it was a living. He would start to work on Monday.

When Ellen came home from her job at the hospital, Rick met her at the door. He almost seemed like the old Rick. He told her about his new job and that they should go out and celebrate.

"We can't go tonight," Ellen said.

"Why not," he said?

"Katie and I have to go to church." she said.

Rick became furious. "You and that church," he said. "You love that church more than you do your own husband."

He did not realize that his little girl was to be baptized that night. She had received Jesus a few months ago but had not yet been baptized. They were having baptism on this Friday because it was a special end to the revival services that had been going on all week.

Rick had been so wrapped up in himself that he hadn't even noticed that Ellen and Katie had been going to services each night. Ellen started to explain but Rick turned and stomped out the door.

Katie came into the room. "Isn't daddy going to go and see me baptized," she said? "I thought you were going to ask him."

Ellen swallowed hard. She really didn't know what to tell her little girl. She just shook her head and said, "No something else came up and he can't."

It was only a little lie. She couldn't tell her precious little girl that she hadn't even gotten to tell him.

They got dressed and went on to church.

Ellen was so proud of her little girl. She looked like an angel. How she longed for Rick to see this. At one time he would have been overjoyed to see his only child baptized, but now he didn't even know it.

A tear fell from her eye.

Things began to get a little better now that Rick had a job. But still Rick seemed to be dealing with something else. When Ellen had explained to him why they could not go out to celebrate that night something happened, but she was not sure what. She felt in her spirit that God was dealing with him, but he just wasn't willing to let go. She and Katie continued to pray.

Rick began to play with Katie like he used to. One day while they were playing ball out in the front yard the ball rolled into the street. Although Katie had been warned time and again not to run into the street, she forgot.

Rick saw the car coming around the corner but he could not get to his little girl in time. The screeching tires sent terror through his spine. He ran to where Katie lay.

Ellen had seen it from the kitchen window. She had picked up the cell phone on her way out and was calling 911.

Katie was not breathing when she got to the street.

Ellen's nursing skill took over and she began CPR. When the ambulance arrived Katie was breathing and there was a pulse, but she was in bad shape.

Ellen went with Katie in the ambulance and Rick followed in the car.

Rick began to pray, "Oh God, please don't let my little girl die. I know I don't have a right to ask but please I love her so much. I am so sorry that I have left you out of my life. Please forgive me of my sin and restore to me the joy of your salvation. I will serve you no matter what, but if it is your will please let Katie live."

Rick felt a peace that he had not felt in a long time. He knew that whatever the outcome he would never again leave God out of his life.

They arrived at the hospital at the same time.

The paramedics rushed Katie into the emergency room. The trauma team was waiting. They rushed her to surgery.

The doctor came out and told the family that they had done all they could do. It was up to a higher power now.

Ellen's pastor and church family had gathered at the hospital. They were holding hands, each one praying for little Katie. The doctor had not given them much hope. Katie was in a coma.

The day turned into night and the night to morning. Weeks passed. There was still no change in Katie's condition.

Rick and Ellen stayed by her bed constantly.

On one such occasion Rick took Ellen's hand and said, "Honey I am sorry for what I have put you through these past couple of years. I may as well say the past 17 years. I haven't been the husband that I should have been. I haven't even been the dad to Katie that I should have been. I was running from God. I didn't want to admit it, but it is true. I knew what God wanted me to do, but I just wasn't willing to give up all I had accumulated. I have asked God to forgive me and He has. If it wasn't for you, Katie would not know Jesus. I should have been the one to lead her to Jesus. I was too wrapped up in myself to see it. If God spares her or even if he doesn't I want you to know that from now on God owns my life; body, mind, soul and spirit."

Ellen knew that he meant what he said. She had seen the change in him in the past few weeks. He was the Rick that she had fallen in love with, the man that loved God more than anything. She was sorry that it took this tragedy to help him see that. After all she and Katie had prayed, "Whatever it takes."

She was thankful God had heard her prayer, although her heart was breaking.

Would Katie be okay?

Everyone continued to pray.

Six months after Katie's accident they were standing by her bed when Katie opened her eyes. Rick and Ellen were beside themselves with joy until Katie spoke.

"Mommy, do you see Him?" Daddy I know you do."

They were puzzled as to what she was asking. They asked her, "Who?"
"Jesus, she said. He is right over there. Can't you see Him?"

Their hearts began to sink within them. They knew that it could only mean one thing. Jesus had come to take her home.

Tears began to spill down their cheeks.

Katie looked at them in puzzlement. "Why are you crying?" she said

They could barely speak but they asked her what Jesus was saying. They could not believe what she said next.

Katie responded "Jesus says that heaven is beautiful, and that one day I can come live there, but now is not the time. He wants me to tell you that we have a lot of work to do, telling people about Him."

With that she gave a big wave and said, "Goodbye, Jesus, I love you too."

Rick and Ellen fell across their young child and sobbed with joy.

It has been 20 years since that glorious day. Katie is about to marry. Her father will perform the ceremony in the small church that he has pastored for 15 years. Her younger brother, Peter will be giving her away. After a short honeymoon, Katie and her new husband will leave for the mission field to tell others about Jesus. All is well.

THE END

RICH THOUGH POOR

Mark 16:26 For what will it profit a man if he gains the whole world and forfeits his soul? Or what shall a man give in return for his soul?
Proverbs 13:7 One pretends to be rich, yet has nothing; another pretends to be poor, yet has great wealth.

The rented moving truck pulled up into the driveway of the big white house with the huge columns. Following it was an old Ford Crown Victoria with rusting fenders and worn tires. Inside the car held the family of William Jenkins, which consisted of his wife, Carolyn and their four children.

Ryan was the oldest. He was 16. He looked a lot like his dad. He was tall with hard muscles in his arms. His dark tan acquired from working the fields made all the girls' heads turn.

Jerry was next. He was 14. He was just as handsome as his older brother but just a little heavier. He liked to eat and never seemed to get enough. His mom called him her human vacuum.

Patty came next, the only girl, she was 13. She was as pretty as the morning sun, just like mother. Her auburn hair was long and naturally curly, not that kinky curly but perfect finger curls that most girls would die for. Her eyes were bluer than the sky, but it was her smile that seemed to captivate everyone around her. She never seemed to be unhappy.

Last but surely not least was the youngest, Jake. He was only 5. He had been a surprise; they thought that they were through having children. They were overjoyed when he came along. He was not as healthy as the other three. His heart had not developed properly, and only beat at half the capacity. Doctor's had told them he probably would not live past his first birthday but so far he had defied all the odds.

There were surgeries but that cost a lot of money, which they didn't have.

They just continued trusting God that He would intervene.

Why was this entourage coming up to this fine mansion?

The mansion belongs to the Stafford's, a very wealthy aristocratic cattle and farm family.

Their huge house has twelve rooms. There are seven bedrooms with a bath in each. There is a stately living room, library, kitchen, dining room, and gym/playroom.

The huge swimming pool in the rear is surrounded by the best of landscaping, with a running water fall and bathhouse.

A little further down the road was the caretaker's house, where the moving truck was headed.

William had been hired to run the ranch. It was the greatest opportunity he had ever had.

He had always been a sharecropper, running other people's farms. They had always been small and the compensation had been small, but there was not a better farmer in all the land.

His family did not have much in material blessings but the love in their little family far outweighed anything that could be found in the big mansion on the hill.

Only time would tell what kind of influence this family would have on the family in the big house.

The vehicles pulled to a stop and the Jenkins family began to pile out.

They could not believe what they were looking at.

Their new home, although much smaller than the mansion, was far better than they had ever lived in before.

 Their homes had always been clean and well kept, their mom saw to that, but they were small and crowded.

This house had four bedrooms and two baths.

 Ryan and Patty would be able to have their own room.

 Jerry and Jake would share a room. Jerry didn't mind. He was always protective of his little brother and that suited him just fine.

They didn't have much furniture but it would have to do for now.

They began to unload the vehicles and carry things inside.

They worked hard all day and everything was in its place. The dishes were even unpacked and put in the cabinets.

Everyone had gotten a bath and dressed in their finest clothes.

Their clothes were not fancy but they were clean.

Carolyn made most of their clothes, especially for her and Patty. Most everything else came from Goodwill or thrift shops.

The kids didn't mind. They were appreciative to get whatever they could.

Their parents had taught them to be thankful for everything God had given them.

They never failed to stop and thank God for what He had given them.

They were a Christian family. They attended church regularly.

William made sure that his kids not only knew about Jesus but that they knew him personally. Even Jake, although he was only five, had made a profession of faith.

William didn't push them he let them make their own decision but when a child sees the love of Jesus in their parents it is only natural that they too would want to know Him.

William read the Bible and prayed with them before the start of each day. He didn't just leave it up to the church to teach his kids.

He wanted them to know all there was to know about God and to learn to depend on Him.

It had paid off.

His kids were not like most kids in today's world. They were well behaved and respectful. They worked hard beside their father and mother without complaining.

You don't see that much anymore. Most kids lay around the house playing video games or hanging around at the mall getting into trouble.

Not so with the Jenkins' kids. They loved to play games as a family and to be with family.

They were different. Before too long they would begin to make a difference to others also.

The plan was for them to attend a big barbeque at the mansion in the evening.

Mr. Stafford was a big man in town. He had invited some of the townspeople to meet his new manager.

They walked up to the big house.

Most of the guests had already arrived and were in little cliques.

As the family approached everyone turned to see them.

Mr. Stafford, who was dressed in cowboy attire with hat and boots, went over to William. He laid his hand on his shoulder and guided him over to the others.

Mr. Stafford said, "I want you to meet my new manager, William Jenkins. This is his wife, Carolyn and their four children."

Everyone casually said, "Hi, glad to meet you." Then turned back to whatever they were doing.

Mr. Stafford took them over to a table where a beautiful woman sat. He introduced her as his wife, Beth.

She held out the tips of her fingers to greet them. It seemed as if she was afraid to touch them. Carolyn just politely took her hand and gave it a good handshake the way she was accustomed.

Beth was dressed in the finest swim attire that money could buy. Her makeup and hair were just so.

Carolyn could not put the two together. Why bother with all of that if you were going swimming.

Little did Carolyn know that Beth never swam when others were present. She was too concerned about her appearance.

Carolyn felt it was going to take a lot to break through that piece of ice. She pushed the thought from her head and took the seat that Mr. Stafford offered her.

Next he took the kids over to where a group of other kids were sitting around the pool.

They heard the kids snicker as they drew near. The snickers quickly died down as they approached.

"This is Ryan, Jerry, Patty and Jake Jenkins," he said.

He motioned to a pretty young girl in a blue bikini."This is my daughter, Amelia. She will introduce you to the other kids."

Amelia rolled her eyes as she often did when her father told her to do something. "Whatever" she said.

Amelia was an only child. She was the same age as Ryan and did think he was pretty cute.

She knew that is as far as it would go. They didn't belong in her circle. Hadn't she and the others been making fun of them just before they came over?

She didn't want for anything but she wasn't happy, as the Jenkins kids would soon learn.

Most of the kids were only her friends because of her dad's money and she knew that.

Their family never did much of anything together. Her dad was not there half the time and her mother was always going to some bridge club or attending a charity affair of some sort. They never had any time for her. She compensated by throwing her dad's money around. Little did they know that she had even tried drugs. She would try anything to hide the pain that she felt inside.

The barbeque ended around 9 and the Jenkins family went back to their new home. They sat down at their kitchen table covered with the red checkered tablecloth.

Their dad began to read from the big Bible they always used for family devotions.

He read from Proverbs 13:7 - **There is he that makes himself rich, yet hath nothing: there is he that makes himself poor, yet hath great riches.**

Little Jake spoke up, "What does that mean, daddy?"

Dad began, "well Jake, it is like this. I guess you noticed all the fine things that the Stafford family has while we were at the barbeque?"

"Yes," Jake said.

Ryan spoke up, "I think I know what you are talking about. They have everything but they don't seem very happy. We don't have much but we are happy and love one another."

Dad nodded his head in agreement with Ryan. "There is more work to do here than tending a ranch," Dad said.

Everyone nodded in agreement. They joined hands and prayed.

It was summer so the kids were out of school. That allowed them to help their dad get things going around the ranch.

They started early each morning and worked hard through the day.

It had been 2 months and things were beginning to fall into place.

The last manager had not done a very good job and there was a lot of work to do.

The kids didn't mind, they enjoyed working beside their father and mother.

They laughed and sang as they worked.

Amelia watched them from her perch on the diving board.

She just could not understand their enthusiasm for work. "Ugh."

It was even beginning to cause more friction between her and her father.

He liked the Jenkins kids and praised them all the time. Why couldn't he praise her?

He never even paid much attention to her except to complain because she wasn't doing anything constructive with her time.

She was going to have to fix this.

She developed a plan. Little did she know her plan would backfire.

She jumped from her perch and ran into the house to get ready.

She was meeting her friends at the mall.

Amelia pulled up into the mall parking lot in her little red sports car.

Her dad had given it to her on her sixteenth birthday.

She was the envy of all her friends. They like to ride around in it and would do almost anything to get a chance to.

She got out and walked into the mall.

Her friends were sitting in the food court waiting on her.

As she walked up they asked her how the "Leave It to Beaver Family" was getting along.

Everybody laughed out loud. It was a running joke with them.

Amelia rolled her eyes. "They are driving me batty, she said. They are such goody two shoes. My dad is always on my case about them. That is why I have come up with a plan to bring them down."

Everyone leaned in close, this they wanted to hear.

Amelia began, "You know the party that we plan to have out at the Jefferson's lake house next week?" Everyone nodded in agreement. "I am going to invite the little angels," "What," they said. "Have you gone crazy?"

"No of course not," she said.

Here is my plan. You know that Rick's parents will not be there. They are in Europe. We plan to have alcoholic beverages and a few other things also. She gave them a wink.

Everyone knew what she was talking about.

Her boyfriend, Carl, who was 21, was going to bring the drinks and smokes. Plus Rick's parents always had plenty of booze around.

The other stuff was being bought by her, from a guy she knew at school.

The kids responded with, "What does that have to do with the angels?"

She responded back, "I figure it this way, when we get them away from their parents then they will let their hair down and become just like us. They are human aren't they?"

Everyone nodded in agreement.

Lori spoke up, "but how are you going to get them there? We haven't been very friendly with them."

"I will tell my dad that I want them to come. He is always trying to get me to pal around with them. Thinks they might rub off on me. My dad thinks we are just having a lake party with Rick's parents present. He doesn't know that they are in Europe. He will ask their dad to let them go and Mr. Jenkins won't be able to say no."

"Great plan," everyone chimed in.

In the preceding weeks, Carolyn had begun to develop a relationship with Beth. She had discovered that she wasn't as cold as she at first appeared. When you got her away from that façade, you could see that she was a lonely, sad person. Who needed a true friend, not just someone who liked her because of her husband's money. She was also searching for something more in her life; that money could not buy.

She and Carolyn had been studying the Bible together and she had begun to attend church with Carolyn's family.

Carolyn felt that it wouldn't be too long before she accepted the Lord Jesus as her savior. Mr. Stafford was a different story. He always asked William questions about why his family was so different but when he tried to talk with him about Jesus, he would just turn him off. He felt that he had everything under control. He didn't need a crutch. That is what he called it, this trusting in Jesus thing.

Carolyn, and Beth tried to get him to go to church with them but he refused.

He didn't mind Beth going, that just wasn't for him.

Amelia refused to go also.

Carolyn and Beth began to pray for them.

Amelia approached her dad regarding the party that was to be held on Saturday.

She knew just how to wrap her dad around her little finger.

She began, "Dad, I was thinking about what you said about the Jenkins kids. I would like to invite them to the party, but I think it would be better of you ask their parents. Would you do that for me?

She turned her head and batted her eyes in that little girlish way that she had used so many times before.

"That is a great idea, he said. I will be sure to tell William this afternoon."

"Thanks dad," she said as she turned and walked away with that sheepish grin that said "gotcha".

Mr. Stafford walked down to the barn where William was giving the thoroughbreds some hay.

"Hey, Jenkins, how is it going?" he said.

Great was William's reply. "What's up?" he said.

"Well Amelia and her friends are going to a party at the Jefferson lake house tomorrow. She wants your three oldest kids to go. How about it?" he said.

"I don't know," William said. "Do you know the Jefferson family?"

"Oh yes, he said, they are a fine upstanding family. Everything will be on the up and up, I am sure."

Little did he know that the parents were not going to be there because they were in Europe.

William responded, "Well I guess it will be alright. Besides the kids have been working pretty hard, a little break with some swimming and good time will do them good. I will tell them that they can go."

The party was to begin at noon, but there were some things that needed to be done before the kids could get away.

It was 3 pm when they finally prepared to leave. Before they left their dad reminded them that they were not only representing their family but they were representing Jesus.

"I trust you, he said, but for some reason I have a bad feeling about this."

Ryan spoke up, "don't worry dad I will take care of us. If things get bad we will just come home."

William knew that his son was telling the truth. He had a maturity about him that amazed even his family.

He had already surrendered his life to Jesus to go into the ministry. He planned to go to Christian college next year when he graduated.

The lake house was about an hour away from the mansion. It took a little longer in the old Ford. It didn't have a lot of power anymore.

They arrived at the lake around 4:30.

As they drove up into the driveway they could hear the loud music, it was deafening even from inside the car.

The kids looked at one another. Ryan stopped the car and they began to get out.

Just then Amelia in her scanty bikini came over. She was holding onto some guy's arm.

It appeared that they were holding one another up.

She had a beer bottle in her hand. Her eyes were glazed over, so were her boyfriend's.

As Ryan surveyed the surroundings he could tell that everyone was in the same shape. As far as he could see there were no adults present.

He stopped where he was.

Amelia spoke up in a slurred voice, "come on over Ryan, the party is just beginning." "I don't think so," was Ryan's reply. I think *we just need to turn around and go back* home."

Amelia shouted out, "Oh go ahead you prude. You are the one that is missing out. You don't fit in here anyway. Go back home to your little sanctuary."

Ryan, Jerry and Patty got back in the car and drove off.

Amelia threw her beer bottle at the car just missing it.

"Oh my goodness, Patty mused; I can't believe what is going on there. Should we tell her parents?"

"I don't know what we will do right now, Ryan said, all I know is that is not where we need to be."

He drove on down the road.

Just as they got to the end of the road that led down to the lake, a sheriff's cruiser raced pass them.

One of the neighbors had called the sheriff's department and reported all the noise and commotion that were taking place over at the lake house. They knew that the Jeffersons were out of the country so they were concerned.

The phone rang at the Stafford mansion. Mr. Stafford picked up the phone and said, "Hello."

"Is this Mr. Stafford?" The voice on the other end said.

"Yes," he replied. What can I do for you?"

He identified himself as being from the sheriff's department.

He explained to him that they had his daughter and her friends in the holding cell. They had been arrested for underage drinking, drugs and disturbing the peace.

Arraignment was set for next week in juvenile court.

If he would come and pick her up they would release Amelia to them until that time.

The other teenager's parents had already been notified.

Mr. Stafford went down to the Jenkins' house. William came to the door.

"I guess you have heard by now," he said.

"Heard what?" he said.

"About our kids being arrested, they did call you didn't they?" he asked. "We have to go and pick our kids up."

"I am sorry to hear that, William replied, but my kids are not there."

Mr. Stafford looked at him with a puzzled look on his face and said, "Didn't they go to the party?"

"Yes, he said, but they didn't stay. They came home when they saw what was going on. I was just getting ready to come and tell you what they told me. I am sorry sir. Is there anything I can do?"

Mr. Stafford hung his head and turned and walked back up the driveway.

He just could not believe this was happening to him. Where had he failed?

Amelia's parents went to the jail and picked her up. There was only silence as they traveled back home. She had tried to come up with a lot of excuses but they knew it was all lies.

They finally told her that they would deal with it when they got home.

She knew that she had gone too far this time.

The arraignment came and went. The judge gave her 3 months probation with 300 hours of community service because it was her first offense.

Her mother and father grounded her for the rest of the summer and took her car keys away. It was late afternoon when they returned from the court appearance. Mr. Stafford didn't go into the house with Beth and Amelia; instead he went down to where William was repairing some fencing.

He just stood there for the longest time watching William and his sons working side by side.

William laid down his hammer and went over to where Mr. Stafford stood. "How did things go?" he asked.

Mr. Stafford explained all that had transpired.

He shook his head and said, "I just can't understand it. I give her everything that she could possibly want. She admitted to me that the only reason she invited your kids was she thought she would be able to bring them down to her level. I guess I just didn't know my daughter after all. I am sorry for what she did but I am grateful that your kids had better sense.

I just don't get it. I thought money could buy everything. I have all the money I could ever want, I give my family everything. Yet we are in a mess.

I look at your family. Pardon me for saying this, but you have so little in comparison. Yet there is more happiness in the corners of this house than in our whole mansion."

William once again began to share with him what made the difference. This time he listened.

He left the house and went back to the mansion.

He had not made a decision yet but he did agree to go to church on Sunday.

Beth was overwhelmed when he told her that they were going to church as a family this Sunday. She slipped away and called Carolyn on the phone and shared the news.

Carolyn told her that she already knew and she suggested they pray and thank God for answering their prayers.

They both bowed their head while on the phone and prayed and thank God. They also ask Him to continue to work in all their hearts.

Heads turned when the Stafford's walked into church on Sunday. No one in that town had ever seen Brad Stafford in church before.

Beth had already been coming with the Jenkins family.
The pastor stood behind the podium and began his sermon.

His sermon was based on Mathew 16:26; **For what will it profit a man if he gains the whole world and forfeits his soul? Or what shall a man give in return for his soul?**

He also used the story of the rich young ruler who came to Jesus.

Brad felt that he was preaching directly to him, although the pastor hadn't even known he was coming.

The pastor continued, "You may have everything that this world has to offer, but your life is empty and in turmoil. Riches cannot buy you happiness. They can't buy you love. And most importantly, they can't buy you salvation and eternal life. Don't you think it is about time that you gave your life to Jesus? He promises to give you life and to give it more abundantly."

The pianist began to play softly and the minister of music began to sing, "Jesus paid It all, all to Him I owe, sin had left a crimson stain, He washed it white as snow." Brad bowed his head; he could feel the tug of the Spirit in his heart. He knew that what he had been doing had not worked; his life was a mess.

His knuckles were turning white from clenching the back of the pew.

The music continued to ring in his ears; along with the Holy Spirit's voice. He seemed to say, "Now is the time, don't wait any longer."

He turned loose of the pew and went forward.

Little did he know that when he did Beth and Amelia would follow.

The whole family gave their lives to the Lord that day. It was a time of great rejoicing.

Four years have passed. The ranch is a different place. There is joy and peace in the Stafford household.

Many of Amelia's friends have come to know the Lord through the witness of her and the Jenkins kids.

Their parties are quite different now.

Things have changed for the Jenkins family also.

Instead of being caretaker for the farm, Brad was so grateful for what had happened to his family that he gave William the house and 20% of the ranch.

He also paid for little Jake's heart surgery. Jake is 9 now and just as healthy as the other kids.

Amelia and Ryan are attending the Christian college, they are going to be married when they finish seminary.

Jerry is in the military and Patty will be graduating this spring. Both of the families know now that life does not consist in the abundance of things but in trusting Jesus Christ, only He can bring life.

THE END

JAILED BUT FREE

John 8:36 So if the Son sets you free, you will be free indeed.
Romans 6:22 But now that you have been set free from sin and have become slaves of God, the fruit you get leads to sanctification and its end, eternal life.

Stacey Reynolds sat on the bunk behind the bars of the state pen. Tears were streaming down her face. What was she doing here? She didn't belong in jail. How had things gone so wrong?

The tragedy of her past life began to play in her mind. She thought back to when she was a child. Life wasn't too bad. Her parents had good jobs. They were not rich but they were better off than some.

While her mother worked she stayed with a baby sitter. She was three years old at the time.

Her baby sitter was Mrs. Jones, the neighbor down the street.

Her 23 year old son, Carl was always around. He didn't have a job and he just laid around the house all the time drinking beer.
All the trouble began then.

Mrs. Jones would often go to the store or someplace, who knows where? She would leave Stacey with Carl. That was a mistake, because he had a thing for little girls. When she would leave Carl would began his abuse.

Stacey did not understand what was going on but she knew she didn't like it.

She couldn't explain to her Mom because of her limited vocabulary and lack of understanding. She would just say, "Carl made boo, boo." Since there was no evidence of any hurt she thought it was just the imagination of her little girl. She never bothered to look into it.

Mrs. Jones was a good baby sitter and took good care of Stacey, plus she was not as expensive as a regular daycare.

She was unaware that she left her alone with Carl almost every day.

This abuse continued until she went to kindergarten and was able to stay in the after school care program. The abuse had stopped but the scars were still there.

While Stacey was in grade school her parents got divorced.

Her dad left without even saying goodbye. She never heard from her dad again.

She and her mom moved to a dingy apartment on the other side of town. Her mom didn't make enough money to live anywhere else.

The neighborhood they lived in wasn't the kind of place you would want to raise a daughter but it was a roof over their heads and didn't cost much.

Since Stacey was 10 her mom felt she could take care of herself after school. Her mom just seemed oblivious to the dangers or just didn't care.

Stacey would run home from the bus stop each day.

Although she was only 10, she had begun to go through puberty. She was unusually tall for her age, and undoubtedly was going to be well developed.

The older boys who hung around her apartment would always whistle and make suggestive remarks as she passed.

She would always rush into her apartment building and up to their apartment as fast as she could and lock the door behind her.

She lived in fear all the time. She had never forgotten what had happened to her when she was little.

Her mother began to bring strange men home with her.

Her mother had changed a lot from the mom she used to know. She just didn't seem to care anymore, about herself or her daughter. Things began to go from bad to worse.

Her mother finally settled for one of the men, his name was Buck. He moved in with them.

Every evening it was the same. Buck and her mom would sit in front of the TV drinking and smoking pot.

Her mother would soon pass out and she would be left with Buck staring at her in a way that made her skin crawl.

Then it happened.

One evening while her mother was passed out Buck came over to where she was sitting. He began to run his hand up the inside of her leg. She pushed him away, but that did not do any good. He grabbed her and took her into the bedroom. He held his hand over her mouth so she couldn't scream. What good would it have done anyway, her mother was passed out. He proceeded to abuse her in the same way that she was abused so many years ago. When he finished he got up and left her laying there crying.

This time she understood what was happening. She had learned a lot for a 10 year old.

The next morning she tried to tell her mother what had happened but her mother wasn't listening. She accused her of being jealous and trying to break them up. She chose not to believe the story and accused her of making it up.

The abuse continued even after her mother discovered him in the act. She just didn't care.

Stacey felt dirty and alone. She didn't know where to turn, until one day a special officer with the sexual abuse unit came to her school. She told the children that it was a crime and not to be afraid to tell someone if that happened to them.

It was then that she got up courage to tell her teacher.

Afterwards the police came to their home and arrested both her mother and Buck.

They charged Buck with sexual child abuse and her mother with accessory after the fact.
Both were sent to jail for a very long time.

This necessitated Stacey being placed with child welfare.

She was placed in foster home after foster home.

A few of those homes were church going people. That was the first time Stacey had ever been to church.

When she heard about the love of Jesus she just became angrier and angrier.

She said, If Jesus loved her, how could He allow everything that had happened to her."

She just couldn't believe that anyone could or would ever love her.

She began to act out in ways that caused these foster parents to send her back to child services. They just couldn't take the chance that she would influence the other kids.

Finally at the age of 15, after having been placed in over 10 different foster homes, she ran away. She lived on the street along with the other homeless people.

She began to sell her body so she could get food and drugs.

She figured that it didn't make any difference. Her life was trashed a long time ago. She endured three abortions during this period and almost overdosed twice. How could her life get any worse?

It did get worse. One day she was in desperate need of a fix. Her regular contact was out of town. So she went looking elsewhere.

A friend of hers told her about a guy over on 7th Street who might have something for her.

She went over there; sure enough there he was on the corner. She approached him and asked if he had any stuff.

He took a package of white powder out of his pocket and handed it to her. She handed him the money. Then all hell broke loose. It turned out that the dealer was an undercover cop and it was all part of a sting operation.

When she went around the corner she was nabbed by two officers in uniform. She was taken to jail. She was released on $10,000 bail until her court date. It was set for the next week.

While she was out she continued her drug use. She was careful from whom she got the fix. She just couldn't get along without it.

She was arraigned in court and in order to get a lesser sentence she pleaded guilty to buying drugs.

She was given a sentence of 5 years in the state facility for women.

The scenario repeated itself in Stacey's mind over and over again.

She even recalled the times that she had attended church with her foster families.

She thought about what the teachers had said about Jesus loving everybody. She just shook her head.

How could anyone love me? I have made too big a mess of my life for anyone to love me. She pushed the thought out of her mind..

Suddenly she came back to the present and realized where she was. She laid down on the hard cot and fell asleep.

In the middle of the night she woke up in a cold sweat. Her stomach was tied in knots. The pain was intense. She ran over to the toilet, where she began to throw up violently. Then the tremors began. Her body shook violently. She laid thrashing around on the cell floor. She was going through withdrawal.

They took her to the infirmary, and put her in detox.

She spent several days there. She wondered how hell could be any worse than what she had gone through.
They took her back to her cell, home sweet home.

The next day came all too soon. She knew that she would not be allowed to stay in the safety of her cell.

She had already been versed on jail life. She had been warned of the dangers and to watch out for herself. The other women prisoners always liked fresh new meat. The thoughts of it made her cringe, hadn't she suffered enough?

The next morning the bell rang and the cell doors opened.

It was time to go to the mess hall for breakfast.

She walked slowly into the hall and went over and picked up her tray and started over to a table.

As she walked pass the other tables the other women prisoners began to whistle and make suggestive remarks. She just kept her head bent low. She surveyed the room. There weren't any places that she could get off to herself. "Over here baby," some of them called out. What was she to do?

Suddenly an older black woman came up. "Over here," she said. "It is going to be okay. We will take care of you; you don't have to be afraid."

She followed the woman with intimidation.
The woman led her over to a table where 5 other prisoners were seated.
The black woman introduced herself as Tamika Willis; then she introduced the others.

"What you in for," She asked?

"Possession of drugs," she answered.

"How much did you get?"

"Five years," she answered. "How about you," Stacey asked?

Tamika's answer startled her. She told her that she was serving life for killing her husband. She had already served 15 years. Tamika noticed the startled look on her face.

"You don't have to worry, she said. I am not dangerous. I just couldn't take the constant beating anymore. So one night while he was passed out drunk, I took one of my butcher knives and slit his throat. My lawyer tried to get me off on self defense but the jury wouldn't buy it. Coming here was the best thing that ever happened to me.

Stacey looked at her in astonishment. How could being put in jail for the rest of your life be the best thing that ever happened?

"I guess that sounds strange to you, doesn't it, Tamika mused. Well you see, if I had not come here I probably would not have come to know my Savior, Jesus Christ."

"Amen," was the reply from the other ladies sitting at the table.

There it was again the name she had heard so long ago. She could not believe it was coming from such a person as this, a person who was going to spend the rest of her life in jail.

"I don't understand," she said.

"Well that is what we hope to help you with," Tamika said. We are here for you and we will keep you safe."

Stacey felt more at ease than she had in a long time. What was the difference in these prisoners? They seemed to be happy even though they were locked up. She just couldn't understand it, but she was drawn to them. She wanted to know their secret.

It was Monday morning and they were seated at the table in mess hall.

Tamika looked at the others and asked, "You think she is ready?"

Everyone nodded in agreement.

"Ready for what," Stacey asked?

"We want you to come to the Bible study tonight," was the reply. We have one every Monday evening. They let us out of our cells for a couple of hours and we get to study the Bible with our leader that comes from the church in Ocala."

Studying the Bible didn't much appeal to Stacey but she thought it would be nice to get out of her cell for a couple of hours and spend some time with her new found friends.

"I will be there," she answered.

Stacey walked into the visitors' room where the Bible study was held. There were probably 20 other prisoners already there. Stacey had not met most of them. She looked around for her friends. There they were on the front row.

They motioned for her to come on down.

She slowly walked down to where they were seated.

The teacher opened her Bible and asked the others to open theirs.

Stacey didn't even own a Bible; she had never in her life even held one in her hand.

The lady got up from where she was sitting and handed her a Bible. "Here, she said, you can have this one. Our church sends these Bibles for those who may not have one. It is yours to keep. We have already cleared it with the authorities."

The kindness in the eyes of the lady made a warm feeling run all through her body.

What was it about these people?

"We have a lot of new girls here tonight," she said. "So I want to go back to basics.

Turn in your Bible to John 3:16."

Tamika helped Stacey find the right place.

The lady began to read. **"For God so loved the world that He gave His only begotten Son, that whoever would believe in Him would not perish but would have eternal life."** She went on to tell how that we are all sinners and that the wages of sin is death, but the gift of God was eternal life through Jesus Christ. How that God even while we were still in our sins sent His Son, Jesus Christ to pay the penalty for our sins.

Stacey's heart tugged within her. Thoughts ran through her mind like wildfire. How could God love someone like her? She had made a mess of everything. She was worthless and no good. Hadn't that been what her mother always said about her? Nobody had ever loved her. How could a holy God love her? And this thing about God being our Father didn't sit very well with her. The only father she ever knew had abandoned her. She still wasn't convinced, but she wanted to know more.

The Bible study ended, but not before the lady told them that there would be a church service on Saturday night. Her pastor and church choir were coming to minister to them. Stacey made note in her mind. She would surely be here.

Saturday night came. All day Stacey was filled with anticipation. She had only been to a couple of church services in her life and that was a long time ago. She did not know what to expect.

The service began with Pastor Phil welcoming everyone to the service. The room was packed.

Stacey figured that most just wanted to get out of their cells.

The choir began to sing. They sang songs about Jesus. Their voices were beautiful but that wasn't what impressed Stacey. They were all filled with happiness and their faces seemed to shine. Was it her imagination?

Pastor Phil got up and began to preach. He once again told of the love of Jesus. He shared his testimony of how his life was in a shamble but Jesus reached down and redeemed him from sin and gave him a new life.

Several amens and hallelujahs came from the audience.

He went on to say that it didn't matter what you had done, Jesus was there to give you a new life.

He is willing to forgive you if only you will let Him.

Pastor Phil closed his Bible and looked out over the prisoners. Stacey felt he was looking straight at her.

Jesus loves you, He wants to save you. Will you give your life to Him today?

Tears began to fall from Stacey's eyes. Could it be true? Could Jesus really love someone like me?

Tamika looked over at Stacey. "He is calling you," she said. Won't you turn your life over to Him? He is waiting with open arms for you.

Stacey got up from her seat and went and took the hand of Pastor Phil.

Stacey could not believe the difference that she felt in her heart. There was a peace that she never knew could exist. She felt a love that she had never known before.

She went back to her cell a new woman. She knew that she was still in jail but she had never felt more freedom in all of her life.

Stacey's time in jail seemed to pass quickly after that. While she was there she had begun to write down her thoughts on paper. She even wrote a book of her life and what Jesus had done for her.

The warden who was also a Christian helped get her book published. The book was selling like wildfire.

She soon would be finished with another. This one was about Tamika and her life. She had a lot to tell the world about what Jesus could do for a life that was submitted to Him.

The day came for Stacey to be released. She could not believe that five years had gone so fast. That morning at breakfast Stacey went around and hugged each and every one of her friends. Some of them would be getting out soon also. She came to Tamika. "I hate to leave you," she said. She knew that Tamika would not get out until Jesus came for her.

"Hush child," Tamika said. This is where God wants me. You know there are a lot more of you coming in here. God wants me to tell them about Jesus also. You go on out into the world and tell those out there. I will do His work in here.

Remember when Jesus sets you free you are free indeed.

Stacey walked through the prison gates into the bright sunshine.

 She turned and looked back at the prison.

She bowed her head and prayed, "Thank you Lord for bringing me here and guide me in my new life. I know things will not be easy but I know you are with me. Amen."

She walked out into the world a new woman.

THE END

THE CONSEQUENCES OF CHOICES

Galatians 6:7-8 Do not be deceived: God is not mocked, for whatever one sows, that will he also reap. For the one who sows to his own flesh will from the flesh reap corruption, but the one who sows to the Spirit will from the Spirit reap eternal life.

Becky slowly walked out the door of the planned pregnancy clinic. Her heart was pounding so hard it felt like it was going to jump out of her chest. It just could not be. She couldn't be pregnant. This was all a bad nightmare. This couldn't be happening to her.

Becky thought back to the previous week when she had taken the pregnancy test in the school restroom. She was hoping it had been a false/positive. Now it was confirmed.

She had come here to Gainesville by herself. She had told her parents that her science class was going on a field trip. It wasn't a lie. They were on a field trip. She just didn't go with them. Oh, she had planned to go for weeks even had the permission slip and everything. She had called her teacher this morning and told her that she was sick. Maybe that was a lie but she couldn't let anyone know where she was going. This was the reason why she came to Gainesville instead of going to the clinic in Ocala. It was less likely that anyone would see her.

She had taken a Greyhound bus up to Gainesville. Luckily there was another one that would return just about the time that the science class would get back.

The bus trip was her only choice. She had only had her license a few weeks and besides she didn't have a car.

She walked back to the bus station. It wasn't far from the clinic. She sat down in a seat in the bus terminal.

She looked around. She didn't think anyone she knew would be taking a bus, but she wasn't sure.

Sure enough there was no one, mostly migrants, probably fruit pickers going to look for work in south Florida. She was relieved.

She just couldn't risk anyone she knew seeing her.

Her family was well known in Ocala. Her father was pastor of one of the churches in town and had been for 20 years. Plus he was heavily involved in politics and the community.

She thought about her family.

Her father, Carl and her mother, Ruth had been married for 40 years.

She had 2 sisters and 2 brothers.

Linda was the oldest, she was 39. She was liked by everyone. She had graduated valedictorian of her graduating class. She was married to the minister of music in their church. They had not had any children, although she wanted a child desperately.

She was a nurse at Ocala Regional Medical Center.

She had never given her parents a minute of trouble growing up. They were always pointing out her attributes to Becky.

Becky resented that but she loved her sister and felt sorry for them because they could not have children.

Carl, Jr. was next, he was 37. He was just like their daddy. He lived in South Carolina with his wife and children. He was the pastor of a small but growing church there.

He was another of her dad's pride and joy.

Faye was next, she was 34. She was not married. She had chosen instead to become a missionary to Indonesia. She was totally sold out to Jesus.

That was okay for Faye, but Becky cringed at the thought. She like boys and wanted lots of children, when the right time came.

Her youngest brother, Jim, was 31. He was attending medical school.

He was engaged to a wonderful girl and they planned to be married when he finished med school.

Then there was Becky. She had been a surprise for her parents. She was what you call a change of life baby. Her mother was 44 when she became pregnant with her.

All the doctors had suggested she have an abortion. "At her age the baby might have serious problems," they said.

Of course that was out of the question. Her parents believed that abortion was murder and a sin against Holy God. They would take their chances.

Becky had been born with no complications. She was perfectly healthy. Everyone in her family doted over her. They were all very protective of their little Becky, as they called her.

Becky was different from the rest of the family. She had not yet embraced the faith they all had. She was not a bad person. She just didn't think it necessary right now.

Things were quite different from when her siblings were young. Her dad was not as strict with her as he had been with her older siblings.

She was allowed to do pretty much what she wanted within limits.

He had stopped family devotions long ago because he had become so busy with the church and his political involvement.

She had not received the same teaching that her older siblings had received. So in her view she had plenty of time. She wanted to have fun.

That thought brought her back to the present time. She remembered where she was and what the clinic doctor had just told her.

He told her that she was just about three months along. He also counseled her that if she wanted an abortion that she needed to do it soon. She pushed that thought from her mind.

Of course she would not have an abortion.

She pondered in her mind as to what she would do next.

She had a date with her boyfriend the next day, which was Saturday.

She would tell him and then they would make plans.

Her boyfriend's name was, Butch. He was the son of one of the church deacons. His dad was a very wealthy man and had a lot of say in the church because of it.

Butch was a senior and would be graduating in a couple of weeks.

He had been a very good quarterback in their school and he had a scholarship to the University of Florida.

They had been dating for about a year.

Becky's parents were old fashioned and would not let her date until she was 15.

Her sisters had had to wait until they were 16.

She was wishing right now that her dad had been as strict with her.

She knew that Butch would understand. He loved her didn't he? She had held out giving up her virginity but Butch had assured her that when you love one another like they did, it would be okay.

He made her feel special. He was always telling her how beautiful and smart she was and that there was no other girl in the entire world for him but her. He told her that it was only right that they prove their love for one another. So she had given in.

They had been careful to use condoms but there was that one time that he forgot to bring any and in the heat of the moment they just couldn't stop.

Besides hadn't he told her that it was unlikely that she would get pregnant. He had been wrong.

The bus ride home seemed to take forever. She had arranged for her girlfriend, Peggy, to pick her up.

Peggy had gone on the field trip and so her parents would be none the wiser that she had not gone on the trip also.

She was glad Peggy had not asked her why she needed to go to Gainesville.

Peggy was waiting when she got off the bus. She drove her home and dropped her off.

She opened the door to their house and walked in.

Her parents were sitting at the dining table having their evening meal.

They asked her how the field trip was.

She said it was interesting but the whole trip had made her not feel well so she was going to bed if they didn't mind.

"Of course," they responded. "We will save you something for later."

She went to her room and fell across the bed.

She dialed Butch's number.

He picked up the phone. "Hello, beautiful" he answered. "How was the field trip?" "It was okay," she said. "I missed you."

"I missed you too, babe. We are going to see each other tomorrow. I can't wait to see you, but I have to go right now. I was just heading out the door."

She hung up the phone. She had hoped to talk for awhile and did not expect his response.

Little did she know what was going to happen tomorrow.

She went to sleep but not a very restful sleep. She tossed and turned all night.

Morning came none too soon for her. She was anxious for evening to come so she could go out with Butch and tell him all she had to tell him.

Butch came and picked her up around 6:00. They were going out to eat and then to a movie, or at least that was what they told her parents.

They always wound up at his uncle's cabin in the woods. His uncle lived in another state and only came to Florida during the winter months. Butch had a key because he was supposed to take care of the place for his uncle.

It made a good place to go to make out.

They arrived at the cabin after picking up a couple of burgers at Wendy's restaurant.

They were seated at the table eating the burgers when Becky spoke up. "I have something important to tell you." She said.

"Hey what gives?" he asked. "You have been moody all the way out here."

She just blurted it out, "I'm pregnant."

"What?" he said. "You can't be.
Whose is it?"

Becky couldn't believe her ears. Was he accusing her of sleeping with someone else?

"Yours of course, she said, how could you even say such a thing?"

"Are you sure?"

"Yes, I went to the planned parenthood clinic in Gainesville yesterday."

"That's good", he responded.

Becky was confused was he saying that he was glad that she was pregnant?

He continued, "You made arrangements to take care of it, didn't you?"

"What do you mean, take care of it?" she asked.

"That is what that place is for you know. It is not really a baby yet. We can just get rid of it and no one will be the wiser." he retorted.

Becky could not believe what she was hearing. How could he think that they would just kill their baby?

"How could you suggest such a thing?" she asked.

"Look, he said, I am not messing up my chances for a scholarship to UF to raise no baby. You should have been more careful."
Becky was devastated. She felt like she was going to throw up.

"You said that we would always be together, that one day we would get married, that I was the only girl for you. I don't understand. This just means that we have to get married sooner than we had planned." She cried.

"I only said those things to get what I wanted. I didn't mean it. You were easy enough." He contorted.

"You have to think rationally," Butch told Becky. "We are too young to take on the responsibility of a baby, even if I wanted to marry you, which I don't. Abortion is the best answer. I will help pay for it. How much does it cost?"

The advisor said that it would be $1000.

"What?" he asked. "I don't have that kind of money."

Becky was relieved. "Then we won't do it," she said.

"Yes we will, I know a guy that my friend used. He only charges $200 and it is right here in Ocala. I can swing that with no problem."

Becky could see there was no getting through to him, he had his mind made up. She didn't have the strength to argue anymore. She agreed it was what they would do. Her heart was breaking.

Butch drove Becky home. He let her out at the curb. He didn't even bother to walk her to the door.

They had decided on their way home he would set up everything for next week. She went into the house and hurried to her room. She didn't want her parents to see she had been crying.

Becky lay in her bed but she could not go to sleep. Everything that had happened tonight kept running through her mind. How could she possibly do what they were planning? Hadn't she been part of picketing the abortion clinics? Now she was going to one and she was going to kill her baby.

Becky went through the weekend like she was a zombie. Her parents thought she was just sick, little did they know what she had planned, and she certainly would never tell them. Or so she thought.

The day came Butch had set up with the doctor for the abortion. It was then that Becky discovered that this so called doctor, wasn't even licensed to practice any more. He did cheap abortions in the back of a dirty abandoned office building.

Becky hesitated but Butch took her by the arm and insisted that they were getting this done today.

Besides he had already paid the quack.

Becky lay on the table after the doctor had performed the abortion. She had seen him just take the pieces of her baby and throw them in a trash can, like it was nothing. She couldn't believe what she had just allowed to be done.

The doctor just walked away. There was no nurse to help her get dressed. There were no instructions as to what she was to do.
She managed to get herself dressed and went into the other room where Butch was waiting.

"Ready to go?" he asked.

Just like that. There was no emotion, no feeling whatsoever, just like she had just had her teeth cleaned.

How could she have been so blind?

Butch took her home and drove off.

She walked into her house.

She was glad that her parents were not at home. She wasn't feeling so good. She went and lay down on her bed and fell asleep.

A couple of hours later she woke up with terrible excruciating pain. She could hardly keep from screaming out in pain.

She managed to pull the covers back. The bed was drenched in her blood.

When she saw the blood, she let out a blood curdling scream. Her parents came running into the room.

Becky's dad ran and dialed 911. Her mother ran to her side. "Becky, what happened?" she cried.

Becky didn't answer. She had passed out.

When the medics arrived they transported Becky to Ocala Regional where her sister worked.

Her sister was waiting in emergency when she arrived. Her sister knew her blood type so they had everything ready.

The transfusion was started immediately.

It was later determined that she had lost at least three pints of blood. She was on the verge of bleeding to death.

Her parents were asked to wait in the waiting area while doctors worked on Becky.

It seemed to take an eternity.
Linda and the doctor came out of the room where Becky lay. Linda seemed to be as white as Becky had been when they brought her in.

"What is wrong with Becky?" they cried.

Linda just hung her head.

The doctor in charged answered. "I am afraid that she is the victim of a botched abortion."

"What, it can't be," Becky's mother cried. She wouldn't do such a thing as that.

"I am afraid it's true," Linda said in a whimper.

They went into the examining room where Becky was. The doctor had admitted her to the hospital but there was no bed yet.

The doctor was afraid there might be danger of infection because of the condition in which the abortion had been performed.

Things were going to be touch and go for awhile.

Becky's parents went over to her bed.

She could not even look them in the face.

"Becky, why didn't you come to us? We would have helped you."

All Becky could say was, "I'm sorry. I killed my baby, I killed my baby."

Over and over again she would say the same thing.

The doctor ordered a sedative for her to calm her down. She was in no condition to answer any questions right now.

While Becky was sleeping her mother slipped out of the room, she needed to make a phone call. It was to her sister, Ellen, who lived in California. She had been there since her college days. The family had disowned her back then because she had an abortion. Things were better now but she chose to stay in California.

Ellen had given her life to the Lord and she was now the director of the program for unwed mothers in Sacramento. She had helped many young girls decide to keep their babies and get them into loving homes with parents who could have no children.

Ruth knew that Ellen could relate to Becky in a way that no one else could.

She dialed the number, Ellen answered.

After hearing what had happened, Ellen said that she would take the next flight out.

Meanwhile they needed to deal with things here and now.

Linda came out to say they were moving Becky to a private room on the OB/GYN floor. She assured her mother she would be away from the nursery area. They did not want to upset Becky any worse than she already was.

After they got Becky settled, her mother and father entered the room. Becky still could not face them.

They questioned her, "Honey, we need to know who the father is. He has to accept responsibility for this also. You are only 16."

Still Becky would not look at them. Little did they know she had been thinking about that ever since she came into the hospital.

She thought about how Butch had treated her, but she still loved him and she knew what would happen to an eighteen year old who had gotten a 16 year old pregnant. Even though it had been consensual, he would be charged with statutory rape and would be arrested. She just shook her head. She couldn't tell them who it was. She would destroy his whole life, and she could not do that even though he had already destroyed hers.

Linda came into the room and encouraged her parents to go down to the cafeteria and get something to eat. She would be close by and keep an eye on Becky.

Linda followed her parents down the hall. She was only gone a few minutes when Butch slipped into the room.

He walked over to her bed where she lay with her face to the wall. He placed his hand on her arm. She sat up startled.

"Oh Butch, I knew you would come," she cried.

He motioned for her to be quiet. "I just wanted to come by and make sure you haven't involved me in this. I will deny it; you know. I have friends who will back me up that you slept around with every Tom, Dick and Harry you could."

Becky could not believe what she was hearing.

He continued, "Look I am sorry all this happened but you know it would destroy my career if they found out it was me. That is the reason I have to do this. You understand don't you?"

"You don't have to worry, Butch, I haven't said anything and I won't. Just get out I never want to see you again." Becky cried.

Little did Butch know Linda had returned to the room and heard every word he had said. He turned and saw her standing there. He rushed passed her and ran out of the hospital.

He ran to the parking lot and got in his car and sped off.

Thoughts were running through his mind like wildfire. "What am I going to do? I can't go to jail. I can't be labeled as a sex offender for the rest on my life. This isn't my fault. She is just as guilty. If she hadn't been such a big flirt I never would have noticed."

Butch just could not bring himself to accept responsibility for his actions. He drove to his house where he went into his dad's gun cabinet and took out his father's handgun and some bullets. He got back into his car and went to the football stadium. He looked around at the field, the stands and score board. He thought about all that he was going to lose. He knelt down on the field and put the gun in his mouth and pulled the trigger.

Becky heard people whispering and crying outside her room.
 She looked over and saw her parents and Butch's parents. Butch's parents looked as though they were going to collapse.

"What is wrong?" she cried out. Everyone looked in her direction. The pain and anguish in their faces told her that something was very wrong.

They walked over to her bed. "Tell me what's wrong," she cried out again. Her dad took her hand. "I am afraid that Butch is dead, he took his own life about an hour ago."

"Oh, God, no." she screamed. "How could all of this happen? It is not supposed to end like this."

They had to give her a sedative to calm her down.

The next day Becky's aunt arrived from California.

Becky turned when she walked into the room. "Oh, Aunt Ellen, my life is over. I have made such a mess. What am I going to do? I want to die also, just like Butch."

Ellen took Becky into her arms. "Don't talk like that, honey. It is going to be okay. Believe me I know how you feel. This is not the end of the world. God loves you and He wants to help you."

Becky shook her head and said, "I don't know how God could ever forgive me after all I have done."

Ellen did not say anymore. She knew that Becky was not yet ready to hear what she had to say. She sat down by her bed and held her hand until she went to sleep.

It had been three days since the botched abortion. Becky didn't' seem to be getting any better.

The doctor came into the room and examined Becky. He read her charts. He went out into the hall where her family was waiting. He told them that she had a severe infection in her uterus and it was necessary to remove it or she would not recover. They had already tried antibiotics to no avail.

They knew it meant she would never have another baby. Tears washed down Becky's face when they told her what was going to take place.

She looked at her dad. She remembered all the sermons that she had heard from the time she was little. She knew what she had done was wrong, but why did she have to suffer so much?

Her dad took her by the hand. She looked into his face and said, "I am sorry dad. I have disgraced God and the whole family, but why is God punishing me so much?"

Her dad lowered his head.

He answered, "I don't know Becky. All sins have consequences, some greater than others. There is a purpose in everything. God loves you and He will forgive you if you ask Him."

Once again Becky just shook her head and said, "How could He ever forgive me?"

When Becky came out of anesthesia after the surgery her aunt Ellen was sitting quietly by her bed. Her parents had gone to get something to eat.

She looked over at her aunt.

Her aunt smiled sweetly and knowingly at her.

Becky began, "Aunt Ellen, you said the other day that you understood how I felt. What did you mean?"

Her aunt began at the beginning. She told her that she too had had an abortion. How the family had disowned her and her struggles with God's forgiveness.

"Did He forgive you?" Becky asked.

"Absolutely, Ellen said with a smile. You see honey that is the reason Jesus died on the cross. He knew we would commit sins and there was nothing we could do for ourselves. There is nothing we could do that is too bad for Jesus to forgive. When we confess our sins, He is faithful to forgive us and to wash us clean. He forgave me and gave me a new life with a new purpose. My experiences have led me to a ministry to help other young women make better decisions. He wants to forgive you also. Don't you want His forgiveness?"

"Oh, yes," cried Becky. Ellen took her hand, "then tell Him. Just confess your sins to Him and ask Him to forgive you."

Becky bowed her head and prayed the sinner's prayer.

Becky returned to school and finished her education, but that was not all. She developed a ministry to young people. She was invited to church youth groups to share her testimony regarding the consequences of premarital sex and out-of-wedlock pregnancies. She told them of God's great love and forgiveness, but how they could avoid the consequences of sin by abstaining from sin in the first place

Her witness and testimony caused many youth to come to Christ and she continues to share her story wherever she goes. To God be the glory.

THE END

UNTIL DEATH DO WE PART

Mathew 19:6 So they are no longer two but one flesh. What therefore God has joined together, let not man separate."
Ephesians 5:33 However, let each one of you love his wife as himself, and let the wife see that she respects her husband.

It was a Saturday morning in mid October. Charlotte stood looking out the kitchen window at the turning leaves. They were beautiful; the red, gold and yellow made it look like a giant tapestry.

She loved this time of year, the cooler weather and the beauty that surrounded her.

This time all she could think of was what was happening to the leaves. They were actually dying. She saw a few fall to the ground. That is how she felt inside. Like she was drying up and dying on the inside.

She went to the kitchen table and sat down and picked up her cup of coffee, and took a sip, ugh, it was cold. She could not stand cold coffee. That was her life cold and dark.

She looked around at the dirty kitchen. She knew she should get up and get busy but she just didn't seem to have any energy. Besides the mess wasn't going anywhere.

The house was awfully quiet.

Her husband, Dan, was off on another hunting trip.

That was the norm for this time of year. Every weekend he would pile in the jeep with his buddies and head out to the woods.

She didn't begrudge him going hunting. The problem was he never had time for her or the girls.

The girls, identical twins, Carla and Kayla, were 13 years old. They had been invited to a weekend camping trip to Blowing Rock. They would not be back until Sunday evening.

It wasn't that she disliked being by herself. Most of the time she would relish having some time alone, but this time it was different. Being alone only gave her time to think about all the things that had happened to her lately.

She and Dan were like strangers in their own home. It seemed they just kept drifting further and further apart.

They had been married for 20 years. She was 24 when they got married. Dan was 28.

The girls came along seven years later.

It had been hard for her to conceive and she had a rough labor and delivery. The doctor suggested that she not have any more children because he felt she would not be able to handle it. So they agreed to have her tubes tied.

She felt Dan resented the fact that he would never have a son. He never said anything but she had known how much he wanted a son. Doesn't every man?

She had also had a problem getting rid of the weight she had gained. She weighed twenty-five more pounds than she did before having the girls. She had tried just about everything to get rid of the weight. It was so hard, it didn't come off as easy as it used to. She was only 44 but she felt like 60 sometimes.

She knew Dan didn't look at her the same way he used to.

Her hair was turning prematurely grey. She felt like an old woman.

It didn't help that he was always making snide remarks about her weight. Or the fact of his staring at all the younger women that walked by with their scantily clad bodies.

Her looks didn't seem to curb his sexual desires. He still had the same sex drive and expected her to be available at his every whim. She felt that it was just for his gratification not because he really desired relations with her. There was never any time to help her get in the mood.

He would hardly speak to her all evening and then when they crawled into bed he expected her to be ready. She felt more like a prostitute than she did a wife. There was no love in their so called love making. She was starved for attention but received little.

Dan was a financial advisor for a large firm and spent a lot of time at the office and the time he wasn't there he spent hunting or fishing.

It had been at least six years since they had been on a vacation together.

She and the girls had gone a few places by themselves, but it just wasn't the same.

At the beginning they would ask why Dad wasn't going, but after awhile they just accepted the fact that he wasn't going to go.

The only outlet she had was her job. She loved her job as manager of a small medical clinic.

Dr. Sam was a good doctor and had been in practice for 45 years. She had worked for him ever since she graduated from college. It was nice working for just one doctor. You didn't have the backbiting that larger clinics had. Plus Dr. Sam was easy going and a jewel to work for.

She was afraid it might soon change. There was another doctor coming to join the practice.

Dr. Sam was getting ready to retire and he was going to sell the practice to a younger doctor.

Dr. Mike would be starting on Monday. She didn't really know what to expect.

That was another thing that was giving her some anxiety. Would he want to keep her after Dr. Sam left?

With that thought she was brought back into the here and now. She got up from the table and began cleaning the kitchen.

She finished all the house work around 3:00 pm.

She surveyed the house.

She felt good that she had gone ahead in spite of her feelings and gotten it done.
All she had left was the laundry. She finished that and put everything away.

She even ironed Dan's shirts. She always did that even though they were permanent press. She just felt that they looked better.

Of course, he didn't seem to notice. No matter what she did, he would find fault one way or another. She just couldn't do anything right.

She pushed the thought from her mind. She decided that she would get in bed and watch the movie she had rented.

It was a romance. Dan wouldn't watch those kinds of movies, chic flicks, he called them.

She enjoyed them when he was gone. She would imagine herself as the heroine of the story. That was the only romance she had in her life anymore. She fell asleep before the ending.

Charlotte got up on Sunday morning and went to church. She enjoyed going to church. She sang in the choir and loved every minute of it. She had the solo part in the choir special today.

The choir finished their anthem and sat down.

The pastor got up and began his sermon.

His message was taken from Ephesians 5:22-33. He was doing a series on "marriage".

How she wished Dan was here. Their marriage could surely use some help.

The pastor talked about the world's view of divorce. He pointed out that the word should not even exist in the vocabulary of a Christian. He went on to say the words, "'til death you part" meant just that. God's word had not changed and it never would. Regardless of the fact over half of the marriages in today's world end in divorce, and the same is true in the church. It didn't mean that a person who was divorced could not be forgiven but that God's best was for two people to remain one for life.

Charlotte knew that he was right. She believed what the Bible said about marriage and in spite of the fact that her marriage had died a long time ago they were still alive and their vows were still binding.

There was one thing for certain. She loved Jesus with all her heart and to please Him was her first priority. Divorce was out of the question.

Dan and the girls returned Sunday evening. They piled their dirty laundry on the laundry room floor.

Her clean house suddenly looked like a war zone.

"What is there to eat?" was the first question out of their mouths, not, "how was your weekend, or we missed you or anything else. "

"I thought we would order a pizza." was her reply.

"What?" Dan yelled. "You have been here all weekend why couldn't you fix us a hot meal?"
"I didn't know what time you would get back," she replied.

"Well I don't want pizza, I am going to go get me a steak," he retorted as he went out the door.

He didn't even ask her if she would like to go.

She ordered the pizza and she and the girls sat around the table and ate it in quietness. The girls knew that she was in a bad mood and didn't want to aggravate the situation.

Dan still wasn't home when they finished their pizza. Charlotte decided to just go on to bed. She was going to have a long day tomorrow.

She was almost asleep when he returned home. He came to bed and reached over for her. She could just pretend she was asleep but that did not do any good. He was determined to have sex. When he finished he just turned over and went to sleep.

She turned her face to the wall and cried herself to sleep.
The next morning came much too soon.

She got up early to fix everyone some breakfast before she left for work.

Dan came in and said, "Why did you make breakfast? Didn't I tell you I have a breakfast meeting?"

"No" she said.

"Well I meant to," was his reply as he went out the door. He turned and said as he was leaving, "By the way, could you see if you could clean up this mess before I get home, this place looks like a pig sty?

It didn't matter that he and the girls were the ones who had made the mess and that she had spent all Saturday cleaning it.

The girls came in and said, "Sorry mom, we are running late no time to eat."

She put the things away and left for the office, she was running late also.

She was hoping that she could beat the doctors there but they were driving up just as she was unlocking the door.

She hurried in before they got out of their cars.

She turned the alarm off and went to her office. She could hear them come in the back door.

The buzzer on her intercom went off. She answered it. "Yes" she said.

Dr. Sam said, "Can you come back a minute. I want you to meet Dr. Mike."

She got up from her desk and went to Dr. Sam's office. She walked into the room. Dr. Sam was seated at his desk.

"I want you to meet my new partner. Charlotte this is Dr. Mike. Dr. Mike this is Charlotte, the best darned office manager in the whole state.

Dr. Mike took her hand. She looked up into his sparklingly blue eyes. She could not believe how good looking he was. It made her blush like a school girl.

Dr. Mike said, "You didn't tell me that she was also beautiful."

Charlotte blushed even more. She felt a familiar tingle go up her spine. She dismissed it as the room being too cold. Deep down she knew that it wasn't that. She was ashamed of the thought that passed through her mind. She was grateful when the receptionist buzzed her that she was needed up front. She quickly excused herself.

Dr. Sam called the receptionist and medical assistant back to his office and introduced them to Dr. Mike.

They came back up front where Charlotte was. All they could say was, "did you see what a hunk he is with that tan and those muscles? He must be at least 6 feet. Wow, he is gorgeous."

She told them to quit acting like silly school girls and get to work. She was trying to hide the fact that she had had the same response. This was one time she was glad she was no longer the medical assistant; she didn't think she could stand working side by side with such a good looking sexy man.

The day went pretty much normal. Dr. Mike had a lot of patients and she did not have to deal with him very much. She was grateful for that. She hoped that she soon would get accustomed to his good looks. She didn't feel that she had anything to worry about on his end since she was six years older than he. She felt men had stopped looking at her long ago. Little did she know what was about to transpire.

The day ended and she went home. When she entered the house Dan met her in the kitchen. "Where have you been? I was expecting this mess to be cleaned up and dinner on the table when I got home."

"There was an accident and I couldn't get through until they cleared it out," she replied.

"Well I am starved, I hope you have something planned," he said.

Luckily she had put out some salmon before she left that morning. She also had gotten some baked potatoes ready and had left instructions for the girls to put them in the oven around 4:00, which they had done. She put the salmon on to cook while she made a salad.

After everyone had finished eating they all got up and went into the TV room. No one offered to help clean up the kitchen. It would have been nice if Dan had at least told the girls to help. They used the excuse of too much homework. She was left alone again to get everything done. By the time she was finished with the kitchen and the mess that they had left yesterday it was time to go to bed. She felt like she would drop any minute.

Before she went to bed she went into the TV room. She tried to get his attention away from the TV but had little success. She needed to tell him something but it would just have to wait.

The next morning she arose early. She went through her closet and pulled out the blue dress that she had bought a couple of weeks ago. It fit her frame nicely and it brought out the blue in her eyes.

She even took time to apply makeup. She didn't usually wear makeup; she didn't really know why she was applying it today.

She sprayed her hair in place and took a look in the mirror. Not half bad she said to herself.

She walked into the kitchen. The rest were up. She had set out some cereal and milk for them for breakfast. Dan had his head stuck in the paper with a cup of coffee in his hand.

She walked over to him and placed her hand on his shoulder. He didn't even look up.

"Dan," she said in a stern voice.

He looked up. "What? he said. Can't you see I am trying to read the paper"

"I just wanted you to know that I will be late tonight. Our new doctor wants me to show him the ropes on our medical billing and dictation system. I may be late every night this week," was her reply.

"I guess you want me to pick something up," he said.

"If you don't mind, it would be a big help."

"Do I have a choice," he asked? She didn't reply.

She went over to the girls and gave them a hug and kiss. "See you later girls."

They looked up and both chimed in together, "Boy mom you look fantastic. Doesn't she daddy?"

Dan just grunted and kept reading his paper.

She went into the garage got in her car and drove off. She was excited about getting to work. She felt like a giddy school girl.

She arrived long before anyone else. She went in and made some coffee. The aroma filled the office.

Dr. Mike was the first to arrive. He had said that he wanted to get there early so they could go over some things. He walked in the door. She was standing in the door of the break room.

He looked her up and down and gave a low whistle. "Boy you look great today. That dress suits you to a tee. I sure do like the scenery around here."

She could feel her face blushing like it did yesterday. She smiled and thanked him.

"That coffee smells great, did you make it," he asked?

She handed him a cup. He took a sip. "That is probably the best cup of coffee I ever had, he said with a grin, beauty and talent all wrapped up in one perfect package."

She chimed. "Why thank you kind sir." Was she actually flirting? She couldn't believe herself. She couldn't remember when the last time was that she felt like this. Was it so wrong? She erased the thought.

She showed him how the dictation program on the computer worked. After that the others began to arrive and the day started as usual. Her doing her job and him doing his. They hardly had time to speak things were so busy. All she could think about was that soon they would be alone again.

The last patient for the day was checked out and the others had left.

She was in her office finishing up some things and he was finishing up his dictation.

Soon he came into where she was sitting. He pulled up a chair next to hers. He put his arm around the chair and placed his hand on her shoulder.

There it was again that tingle, only this time it was stronger. She was simply going to have to turn the thermostat up some. She was lying to herself, it had nothing to do with the temperature in the room and she knew it.

He leaned in closer. She could feel his warm breath on her face. Now the room was getting hotter. What was with the temperature all of a sudden? It was all she could do to show him what he needed to know about the system. They finished around 8:00.

"Why don't we go grab a bite to eat," he asked?

"No, I can't." was her reply. It is much later than I expected I should be getting home. The girls will be concerned. She hardly gave Dan a thought.

Dan as usual was watching TV when she got home. He never even acknowledged that she was home. She went to the girl's room and kissed them goodnight and went and took a cold shower.

The next morning when she arrived at the office there was a vase with three yellow roses sitting on her desk.

She read the card. Thanks for helping me with the computer program. I don't know what I would do without you. I hope you like roses. It was signed Mike. She smiled and held the roses to her nose. The fragrance was breathtaking.

She couldn't remember the last time Dan had given her flowers or anything else for that matter. Not even on their anniversary or her birthday. A card would have been nice. His excuse was always that he didn't have time to pick one up. It was funny that he had time to get whatever he needed for his hunting trips. She knew she just didn't matter to him anymore.

The only time that he said I love you was when she asked or in response to her saying I love you. She often wondered, "does he really love me?"

He sure did very little to show her. She put the roses to her nose once again and breathed in the rich fragrance. She thought of the time that they had spent together in the office last night.

Then she heard it that warning voice in her head. She had heard it on that first day but she chose to ignore it. She hadn't done anything wrong, or at least she didn't think so. Still there it was, why couldn't she shake it?

When Dr. Mike came in she went into his office.

"I want to thank you for the flowers," she said. " I love roses. Oh heck, I love all flowers. They were so beautiful." "Beautiful flowers for a beautiful woman," he said with a wink. "I just like to show my appreciation for a job well done. Have you got a minute?"

"Sure," she replied. "What's up?"

He proceeded to tell her about the medical convention that was to take place next week. He explained that there was a special session for office managers and he would like for her to go with him. He knew that she was well versed but it never hurt to hone up on the newest techniques.

"How long is the convention," she asked?

"It is from Friday through Sunday morning. We would go up on Friday morning and return Sunday afternoon. Of course, the office will pick up the tab. Do you think you can go?"

"I will pass it by my husband." She replied.

There is was again, that warning feeling in the deepest depth of her soul. She once again pushed it aside.

"What could it hurt?" she asked herself.

She knew better. Her pastor had just preached on the dangers of a man and a woman being alone together. She rationalized it by telling herself that they would be at a convention with several thousand other people. What could possibly happen?

She planned to pass it by Dan that night.

She got home a little early so she fixed Dan's favorite meal. She had it ready when he got home.

"Smells great in here, he said. What's the occasion?"

"Nothing, I just got home early so I had time to make dinner. I thought you would like a nice home cooked meal for a change."

She knew she had lied. She had a motive for this meal and she knew it.

They sat down to eat.

She began, "Oh, by the way there is a medical convention this weekend. Dr. Mike wants me to go because there is a special session for office managers. He says that I will be able to hone up on the newest managing techniques."

She waited for a reply. "Sounds great to me, besides me and the guys are going hunting. What about the girls?"

"They are having another sleep over at Kay's house," she replied.

"Then it sounds like it is all set," he said.

"I guess so. It will be just me and Dr. Mike going. Does that make any difference in how you feel?" she asked.

"Why should it?" he replied. I trust you, besides didn't you say that he is six years younger than you. I don't think I have anything to worry about."

It felt like he had just slapped her in the face. One minute he was saying he trusted her and in the same breath as much as said that he didn't think Dr. Mike could possibly have any interest in her. At least that is how she took it.

"Then it is settled, I will go," she said.

Thursday evening Charlotte packed for the trip. She put in her business suit for Friday evening and her slacks and silk blouse for Saturday's session. Then she took out the black satin dinner dress that she had bought for the banquet on Saturday night. It had thin straps with tight fitting bodice with a skirt that flowed in the breeze. It was not anything like the usual dress she would wear. She didn't even know what possessed her to buy it, but it made her feel young and sexy. She packed her black satin heels and closed the case. What was she doing? Had she lost her mind?

The next morning she put her luggage in Dan's car. He was going to drive her to work because she and Mike were going to drive over to the convention together. It was only a couple of hours away to Asheville where the convention was to be held.

They arrived at the office before anyone else. Dan got out and got her luggage out for her. He set it inside the office and turned to leave.

She put her arms around his neck and held on. "I love you," she said.

"I love you too," he replied. In the same moment he was prying her arms from around his neck. "You would think you were leaving forever," he retorted. "I have to get going. Have fun. I will see you Sunday."

She stood for the longest watching after the car. She wished she was going back home with him.

She could not shake the bad feeling in the pit of her stomach.

"Oh, get hold of yourself," she thought. Everything is going to be alright."

Dr. Mike arrived 15 minutes later in his red sports car. "Are you ready," he asked?

"Yes," she replied, I guess so."

"By the way you look great as usual," he said as he put the luggage in the trunk.

He opened the door for her. She got in and they sped off.

The ride through the mountains was breathtaking. The leaves were at their peak.

The wind blowing through her long hair made her feel like a teenager again. She was in ecstasy.

They arrived at the hotel convention center at around 10:00 am. They both got registered and picked up all their materials. They went to their rooms to unpack. It turned out that their rooms were side by side.

At 4:30 a knock came at the door. She opened the door. She had changed into her red suit with the white satin blouse and matching shoes.

"Boy you look better every time I see you," he said. "I can't wait until tomorrow to see what you have for the convention."

"Oh, get real," she said shyly.

"No, I mean it," he retorted. "You are a really beautiful woman and I am glad to be your escort to the grand ball. I will be the envy of all the other guys."

She laughed giddily like a young school girl. He took her arm and they went down to the area where dinner was to be served. They each had steak, baked potato and salad. She had a glass of iced tea and he a glass of wine.

Mike checked his watch. It was time to go to the first session, since this session did not apply to her she opted out by saying she was tired and needed to check in early.

She left him at the entrance to the meeting room. "I will see you tomorrow," she said.

"How about a night cap later," he asked?

"I don't think so. It has been a long day and the session will not be over until 10:00, I will see you tomorrow." she pleaded.

"Okay, tomorrow it is," he said.
With that she walked back to her room. She was relieved that she would not have to deal with anything else tonight.

The next morning Mike knocked on her door.

"You ready," he said.

"Yes, I will there in a minute," she answered. She took one last look in the mirror. Her navy slacks and white silk blouse made her look great, or at least she hoped he would think so.

She opened the door. "Wow," he said. "I didn't think it could get any better but it has."

"Oh, stop," she said.

She didn't really mean it. She was enjoying all the attention. It had been so long since anyone paid her any attention.

They went to breakfast and then they parted ways and went to their separate sessions. It had been agreed they would not wait on each other but would come back to their rooms whenever they were finished and get ready for the banquet. They agreed on 6:30 pm. The banquet started at 7:00.

It was 6:20. Charlotte gave herself another once over. She couldn't get over how she looked. She actually thought she looked great. She was wondering how Mike would view her. She already knew the answer to that.

Her little black dress showed a little more cleavage than she was accustomed. She justified it by the fact that most all the dresses were made like that these days. What was a woman to do? Besides she had her lace shawl to cover up with. She wrapped it around her shoulders and went to the door because Mike was knocking.

When she stepped out into the hall, he pretended like he was about to swoon. She hit him on the shoulder and laughed.

He didn't look half bad in his tux. She felt like Cinderella with the handsome prince.

There it was again, that warning feeling. She just ignored it and took his arm.
The meal was delicious. They had enjoyed every morsel. They didn't eat the desert; maybe they would have some later.

Now it was time for the band to begin. Mike asked if she wanted to dance.

She thought about it for only a few moments. She loved to dance but never got to because Dan didn't like to dance. So anytime they went anywhere where there was dancing, she just had to sit and watch. She knew that it was not right for her to dance with anyone but her husband, but what could it hurt? She was glad that it was upbeat music. She took his outstretched hand and started for the dance floor.

She wrapped her shawl closer around her, but just as she was about to get up Mike took the back of the shawl and said, "why don't you just leave that here? It will be a lot easier to dance."

She let the shawl fall to the back of the chair, revealing her tanned shoulders and the cleavage that she was so desperately trying to hide. "There that's better," he said.

They danced the twist and mashed potato. Mike was a good dancer. He had a lot of rhythm. She was having the time of her life. She was hoping it would not end soon.

The band began to play a slow tune. She started back to her seat. She knew it certainly would not be right.

He took her by the arm and pulled her close. "Oh, no you don't," he said. I have been waiting for this all night."

He pulled her close and they began to sway with the soft music. She could feel her body melting into his. She laid her head on his shoulder and savored the moment.

The banquet ended at 11:00 pm. They walked arm in arm back to their rooms.

"I don't know how long it has been since I had such a good time," she whispered. "I hate for it to end."

"It doesn't have to," he chimed in. "How about us ordering some coffee and desert and having it sent to your room? We need to talk over the plans for tomorrow."

She hesitated only for a moment. Against her better judgment, she said, "Okay."

They walked into her room and shut the door. They called room service and ordered the coffee and pie.

He took the shawl and hung it over the chair.

The waiter brought their order. Mike gave him a $10 bill and he left.

They finished the desert at the table and went and sat on the little love seat next to the open window.

They had full few of the full moon up in the star lit sky.

What a perfect view she thought.

He reached over and began to run the tips of his fingers over her bare shoulders.

"I can't get over how beautiful you are," he whispered as he leaned in closer. I don't think you know what you do to me. Ever since I first saw you I have wanted you. I don't think you know how you make me feel."

He took her chin in his hand and looked into her eyes. Then it happened. He bent down and softly kissed her on the lips. Then he took her in his arms and began to kiss her passionately. Her heart felt like it was coming out of her chest. Her body tingled with excitement. He took his right hand and slid the strap of her dress down off her shoulder and reached behind her and began to unzip her dress.

Then there it was that voice in her head and heart. Louder than ever this time. "STOP, DON'T, YOU CAN NOT DO THIS"

She took both her hands and pushed him away. "Get out," she cried. I can't do this, it is wrong."

He got up from the loveseat. "Then why did you lead me on," he said accusingly.

"I didn't, I didn't mean to, I am so sorry," she cried. "Please leave."

He left the room and slammed the door behind him. She went over and locked it and placed the chain in the slot.

She fell down on her face on the floor.

"Oh, Lord what have I done? Please forgive me. I have sinned against you and my family. How can I ever forgive myself or asked Dan's forgiveness? Please forgive me." She sobbed and sobbed.

Then she heard it again but this time it was a still small voice. I have forgiven you and will continue to do so. I am your Father and I love you. If you had listened to me the first time you would not be in this mess.

She knew He was right. He had warned her several times but she was too wrapped up in the romance of it all to listen.

She got up from the floor and went and took a shower. She felt dirty and unclean. Thank God that she was able to finally listen to His Spirit before it was too late.

She got up early the next morning and went to the lobby and checked out. She ordered a rental car and went outside to wait.

She didn't want to have to see Mike before she left. She didn't know what to say. All she knew was that when she got back to the office she would hand in her resignation.

The rental place picked her up and she took them back to the office. She filled out all the paper work and started the long drive home.

What was she going to say to Dan? How was he going to deal with this? She was not looking forward to looking him in the face. Would he forgive her, would he leave?

The Lord had told her to leave it in His hands, but still she could not shake the fear and trembling in her very soul.

Would Dan use this as an excuse to get out of the marriage? She had been unfaithful. He would be scripturally justified.

The thought overwhelmed her. She loved Dan and always would, but she just didn't know whether or not he loved her. I guess now is the time that she would find out.

She didn't expect to find Dan at home, but he was. She walked into the house. He looked up from the paper when she walked in. "What are you doing home so early," he asked? "I thought it wasn't over until later."

She didn't readily answer him but asked him the same question. "I had the strangest feeling that I needed to get home fast. So I did," he answered.

Tears began to fall down her face.

Dan got up from his chair and came over and put his arms around her. "Chicky, what's wrong," he asked? He hadn't called her that in years. That had been his pet name for her when they first married.

She began to sob uncontrollably. "I am so sorry, can you ever forgive me?" she cried.

"Forgive you for what?" he asked.

Then she began at the beginning and told him the whole sordid story. All that had happened the last two weeks up to last night.

When she finished she just sat there waiting for the outburst, but it didn't come. His face looked as drained and ashen as she felt.

"Say something," she pleaded.

He got up and walked over to the window and looked out over the lawn. He stood there for what seemed like an eternity to Charlotte.

She spoke first, "I can understand if you can't forgive me but please say something."

He turned slowly and looked at her. He began, "It is I who need forgiving. The Lord has been convicting me of the fact that I have been neglecting you. I have been taking you for granted for so long. I really don't know why you have stayed with me. I was so wrapped up in my own things, I forgot that you have needs also."

He lowered his head.

Charlotte went over and put her arms around him and said, "We both need forgiveness," she said, "not just from each other but most of all from our Lord and Savior, Jesus Christ. It is Him we have sinned against."

They went into their bedroom and knelt down by the bed and poured out their hearts to the Savior.

When they had ended their prayers they arose from their knees, feeling like new creations. They knew that everything was going to be alright.

They got ready to go to church they didn't want to miss the next sermon in a series on marriage, If anyone needed it they did.

They both decided that she would hand in her resignation on Monday. She told Dr. Sam that she had to for personal reasons. She was sorry she could not give a proper notice but it was best to end it like this. She did not bring Dr. Mike into the picture at all. That would not be necessary.

She had trained her assistant well and she could take over for her with no problem. It would not be a difficult transition for them.

She was thankful that Dr. Mike had to go by the hospital before he came to the office. That way she would not have to face him. She did not want to just leave it hanging so she wrote a short note.

> Dear Dr. Mike,
>
> I could not leave without telling you how sorry I am for all that happened. I should have stopped it long before I did. I hope you will be able to forgive me. I am a Christian and I knew better. My moment of weakness hurt us both. I think it best that I leave the practice for the sake of us all.
>
> Sincerely, Charlotte

She placed the note on his desk and walked out the door, never to look back again.

Charlotte and Dan decided that they would renew their vows. It would be a perfect ending to the marriage enrichment series that pastor was about to conclude.

The years came and went quickly after that. Their marriage wasn't a perfect marriage, there was no such thing, but it was a good marriage.

They learned to better communicate and spend more time with one another. They didn't take one another for granted.

They watched their daughters grow up and get married and have children of their own. They even had great grand children.

They traveled and visited places that she had only dreamed about before. They enjoyed life together.

Today was a very sad day for Dan. His beautiful wife of sixty years passed away a few days before and today is her funeral.

He stood before her casket with tears in his eyes. I love you my darling. I hope you knew that. We

made it didn't we? "Until death do we part," we kept our promise to God and each other.
I was hoping I would go first. God always knows best though. I know it is not good bye for long, I will see you on the other side very soon; wait for me on the shore by the crystal river. He bent down and kissed her cold cheek. Good bye "Chicky" I will see you soon."

With that they closed the casket and he went to his seat beside his daughters and their families.

The pianist began to play "Amazing Grace".

THE END

NEVER TOO OLD

Psalm 71:18 So even to old age and gray hairs, O God, do not forsake me, until I proclaim your might to another generation, your power to all those to come. Isaiah 46:4 even to your old age I am he, and to gray hairs I will carry you. I have made, and I will bear; I will carry and will save.

She looked in the mirror and staring back at her was someone she hardly recognized. A woman with white hair and "thank the Lord" not too many wrinkles.

What happened to the young girl that she once knew? It seems like an eternity but then again only yesterday, that she was young and vibrant.

Where did the wonderful dreams go she had hoped to achieve? What had she done with her life?

She stood there staring at herself in the mirror. She began to contemplate the past 62 years of her life.

Growing up in a minister's family wasn't easy. Times were often hard. People often expected things of preacher's kids that they would not expect of their own.

Her dad was a strict disciplinarian. He would often preach at them instead of encouraging them. She supposed that he expected more of them than the church members did.

In spite of it all; she loved her Dad with all her heart. She loved what and who he stood for even more.

He just wanted us to love and honor the Lord. He was so afraid that we would envelope the lifestyle from which he had come before the Lord saved him.

On the contrary, she had chosen to travel the same road that he was travelling. Her life's purpose was to serve and follow the Lord.

"Had she done that?" She asked herself.

She wondered what would happen when she stood before the Lord, would He say well done my good and faithful servant, or would she hang her head in shame.

She had tried to be obedient and follow the Lord's leading. There was so much she wanted to do; but here she was, her life was almost over. What had she done of any lasting value?

Suddenly her mind was brought back to the present. She continued to stare at herself in the mirror.

"Maybe if I started coloring it again," she thought. It would make me look younger and people would not think that I was too old.

That is how she felt sometimes, like she had lost her chance.

"It is time for the younger ones to take over," she mused. "I missed the opportunity to do anything great."

Suddenly she heard the voice of the Lord say, "think about some of the great heroes of the Bible, how old were them?"

She reached into the recesses of her mind and began to remember patriarchs of old. There was Abraham who was 75 years old when God called him out. Moses was 80 when he had his burning bush experience; Joshua and Caleb were 80 when they took the Promised Land.

Then she recalled a scripture that she had read. She picked up her Bible and turned to Isaiah 46:4. There it was the promise that God had given to her on her sixtieth birthday.

She had been feeling particularly low at the prospect of turning 60.

The devotions for that day were taken from this passage. The scripture reminded her of how God had carried her from the womb and that He would still carry her into old age.

Then in another passage she had read, He who has begun a good work in you will finish it. (Philippians 1:6)

It was as though God said, "I am not finished with you yet, I have only just begun.

She knew that her white hair didn't mean she was washed up. It just meant that she had a little more experience than most. God was still in control and still had a purpose for her. When He was through with her, He would take her home. She needed to get busy.

The End

MANSION ON A HILL

John 14:2 In My Father's house are many mansions; if it were not so, I would have told you. I go to prepare a place for you.
I Corinthians 2:9 But as it is written: "Eye has not seen, nor ear heard, Nor have entered into the heart of man The things which God has prepared for those who love Him."

I can feel my heart racing as I travel up the winding road, pass the beautiful green rolling hills.

I can hardly believe that the time has finally come. I have been dreaming of this for years. I have always been able to see it in my mind or at least I thought I had.

My mind could not even imagine nor have my eyes ever seen such beauty. If is far greater than I ever imagined.

I pass the tall green trees with the white fences. Horses are grazing in the lush green fields.

The blue skies with the white floating clouds are beyond imagination.

I go a little further up the road and there it is. My dream home on the top of a hill with a well manicured green lawn.

The view is exhilarating. It takes my breath away.

I turn up the winding driveway. It is lined with dogwood trees in full bloom. Such beauty I have never seen.

The well landscaped green lawn has flowers of all kinds swaying in the breeze. Daffodils, roses, lilacs, you name it, the fragrance mingles together, tantalizing the nostrils.

The fruit trees with all kinds of fruit grace the property, my mouth waters from the thought of it.

Finally, I reach the house. It is much bigger than I had imagined. The huge wraparound porch with tall stately rocking chairs; I am tempted to just sit awhile. No, I can't, I have to see the inside.

I walk through the open door. There is no need for doors to be closed here. This neighborhood is like no other in which I have lived. There is no fear of crime.

I look around. I can see my reflection in the shining hard wood floors. The ornamental rugs are beautiful. The furniture is so magnificent. The art work seems to tell my lives' story. I am amazed.

I hear a faint cry. I enter the nursery. There lays my tiny son. I pick him up. It has been so long. He is so tiny, but he is the spitting image of his older brother and younger sister when they were babies.

His big blue eyes and the tiny wisps of blond hair, there is no doubt to whom he belongs. I bend down and kiss his tiny forehead as I did his older brother so many years ago. He smiles that little baby smile. I hold him tightly in my arms.

All of a sudden I hear this beautiful music. The melody is more beautiful than I have ever heard. I sing along. I am surprised with my own voice. It is simply beautiful. I sing with zest. There is no one bothered by my singing.

I go back out on the front porch. I sit down in the big rocking chair. It is almost time for the family reunion. I can hardly wait to see Mom and Dad, my in-laws, my grandparents and all my aunts and uncles. Oh yes, and the very special guest.

There they come. I can see them coming up the long driveway.

I look up and the special guest is standing in front of me. He looks at me with those eyes of compassion, that tender loving smile. He takes me into his arms and says, "Welcome to your new home, my sister". I in return say, "thank you Lord."

.

The doctor turns off the defibrillator and notes the flat line on the heart monitor.

He turns to the nurse and says, "time of death 2:42pm." I will go and notify the family.

He enters the room of anxiously waiting family and friends.

They know immediately what he is going to say. "I am sorry but she did not make it, she is gone."

The family begins to cry. The daughter can hardly bear it. Her father takes her into his arms and holds her tightly. He then softly says, "Don't cry my precious daughter, our hearts are breaking it is true. She is in a better place; she is where she has always dreamed of being. Your mama is "finally home."

The End

A Note From the Author

Dear Readers:

I hope you have enjoyed reading my book.

My purpose for writing these stories is to help you see that God loves you and He is willing to forgive you when you ask His forgiveness.

Jesus died on the cross to take care of all your sins.

He is the only way to God the Father. There is no other way.

I know that I am not politically correct in saying this but I am telling you the truth.

You may choose to believe or not, God gave you that right.

The choice you make means the difference in heaven or hell. You choose. Where do you want to spend eternity?

Here are some scripture to help you to find life.

Romans 3:23 For all have sinned and come short of the glory of God; Romans 6:23 For the wages of sin is death but the gift of God is eternal life through Jesus Christ our Lord Romans 10:9-10; 13; That if you will confess with your mouth the Lord Jesus and believe in your heart that God raised Him from the dead, you will be saved. For with the mouth confession is made unto salvation and with the heart man believes unto righteousness, 13. For whosoever calls upon the name of the Lord shall be saved; John 3:16 For God so loved the world that He gave His only begotten son that whosoever believes in Him should not perish but have everlasting life; Acts 16:31 Believe on the Lord Jesus Christ and who shall be saved and your house.; Ephesians 2:8-9 For by grace you are saved through faith and that not of yourself, it is a gift of God, not of works lest any man should boast.

My prayer is that you will come to Jesus. He is waiting for you to open the door, Revelation 3:20 Behold I stand at the door and knock, if any man hears my voice and opens the door I will come in to him and dine with him and he with Me.

If you have made a decision to follow Christ, please contact me at the address on the back of the book.

If you enjoyed this book, let others know.

In Jesus Name,

Joan Gasperson

References for "No Other Way"

The New King James Version of the Bible

The Declaration of Independence

The Bill of Rights

Allaboutreligion.org

Wikipedia.org

Hinduwebsite.com

Islamreligion.com

Scripture passages taken from the New King James version of the Bible. Author, God the Father. 2 Timothy 3:[16] All Scripture *is* given by inspiration of God, and *is* profitable for doctrine, for reproof, for correction, for instruction in righteousness, [17] that the man of God may be complete, thoroughly equipped for every good work.

www.ingramcontent.com/pod-product-compliance
Lightning Source LLC
Chambersburg PA
CBHW061647040426
42446CB00010B/1617